INSIDERS

WOMEN'S EXPERIENCE OF PRISON

Una Padel
and
Prue Stevenson

To Sarah Hewer, who died in Pucklechurch Remand Centre
on 12 January 1985, aged 21

Published by VIRAGO PRESS Limited 1988
41 William IV Street, London WC2N 4DB

Copyright © Una Padel and Prue Stevenson 1988

British Library Cataloguing in Publication Data
Stevenson, Prue
    Insiders: Women's experience of prison
    1. Women prisoners—England
    I. Title   II. Padel, Una
    365'.43'0942   HV9647

    ISBN 0-86068-867-4

Typeset by Florencetype Limited of Kewstoke, Avon
Printed in Great Britain
by Cox & Wyman Limited of Reading, Berkshire

Contents

Acknowledgements

This book was possible only because the women whose stories are told here were prepared to expose their lives to public scrutiny and to talk about difficult and painful episodes, most of which they would have preferred to put behind them and forget. They were also prepared to take the risk of recognition and consequent hostility. We therefore give special thanks to Adaku, Ginger, Janet, Jean, Joanne, Lee, Margy, Martia, Mary, Sharon and Sue, and to all the other women we spoke to but whose accounts we were unable to include. We would like to thank them not only for laying themselves on the line but also for their comments and advice on the shaping of the entire book.

Our thanks are due as well to Cath Ginty for many hours spent on the word processor; to Jean Macpherson, Leila Barclay and Sue Trevelyan who helped with the typing and gave advice; to Olga Heaven, Jenny Hicks, Sigrid Padel, Stephen Shaw and Chris Tchaikovsky for fruitful discussion and guidance, and special thanks to Jane Parkin from Virago for her skilful and sensitive editing.

Introduction

Women's prisons are secret places, hidden from public view. Although terrifying reports about the psychiatric unit at Holloway prison or about kangaroo courts at Styal occasionally hit the headlines, most of us remain largely unaware of what really happens behind the prison walls. Myths flourish, fanned by the male-dominated media always on the lookout for a salacious story. The truth is very different – and far more outrageous. By presenting the first-hand accounts of women who really know what prison life is like, this book attempts to put the record straight. It concentrates on the experiences of women who have spent time in prison for crimes which were not overtly political and who do not have access to the usual channels of communication. Their voices are seldom, if ever, heard.

The women with whom we spoke, and whose stories are here told in their own words, come from a wide variety of backgrounds, and they describe an equally large range of experiences. They include Black, other ethnic minority and white women; women who have served short sentences and those who have been in prison for longer periods; young and older women; lesbian women and heterosexual women; women with and without children. Their stories are not limited to descriptions of prison life – for some prison was a terrible shock, unlike anything experienced before; for others it was yet another institution, different only in detail from the children's homes and approved schools they had already lived in. Most of the women speak of their lives before their imprisonment, putting the meaning of their time in prison into a personal context. All speak of the devastating after-effects.

As in any institution, but far more than in most, prison life is dominated by rules, regulations and procedures. The pettiness, the injustice and the arbitrary use of power associated with these rules are brought out in the women's accounts. In this introduction we set out the background to women's imprisonment and describe the general regime that governs prison life.

Britain imprisons proportionately more people than any other country in western Europe. This high prison population includes about 2,000 women and girls currently in prisons in England, Wales, Scotland and Northern Ireland. Approximately 8,600 pass through the prison system each year.

Many of the women who are in prison are on remand, either waiting to go to court or awaiting sentence. They will in almost every case be held in prison for several weeks; sometimes they will be held for months. In 1986, out of the 3,676 women and girls who were remanded in custody in England and Wales, 65 per cent were either acquitted or did not receive a custodial sentence when they were eventually tried. Of those who were sentenced to prison in that year, over 60 per cent were convicted of offences involving theft or fraud – usually shoplifting, DHSS fraud or using stolen chequebooks and credit cards. Fewer than 10 per cent were imprisoned for offences involving violence. Almost half the women who passed through prison in 1986 did so because they had failed to pay a fine. Although soliciting for the purpose of prostitution is no longer an imprisonable offence in its own right, magistrates often fine women extremely large sums for soliciting. These women are either forced to return to the streets to earn enough money to pay the fine or face imprisonment for defaulting on payment. Other women, fined for failing to have a TV licence, or for a multitude of other offences not deemed to warrant a prison sentence at the time of conviction, may also end up in prison simply because they cannot afford to pay the fine.

There is a disproportionate number of Black and other ethnic minority women in prison. A study done in 1986 by NACRO showed that out of the total number of women sent to prison in 1984, 18 per cent were Afro-Caribbean women, who make up only 5 per cent of the female population overall. Such figures suggest that Black women are more likely to be apprehended by the police and are judged more harshly by our predominantly white magistrates and judges. There are also a number of women in prison who are foreign nationals, particularly women from Africa, Latin America and Asia, some of whom are serving long sentences for drug importation. Many do not speak English. They may have children in their country of origin and no friends or relatives in this country. The problems facing these women are particularly acute.

The majority of women in prison are in their twenties, but ages range from fifteen to over seventy. In 1984, women were imprisoned for an average of 340 days, and each cost the state £344 per week at the time of writing.

As women constitute only 3 per cent of the total prison population, there are far fewer prisons to accommodate them. There are twelve in England and Wales, one in Scotland and one in Northern Ireland. (See Appendix I for list and description of each prison.) Six are 'closed' or secure prisons with high walls, electronic gates and locked doors. All are heavily shielded from public scrutiny. Over recent years television cameras and journalists have been permitted selective access, but this is still entirely on terms dictated by the Prison Department. All prison staff are subject to the Official Secrets Act, and although it is doubtful whether any prosecutions would result from current or past employees speaking out on conditions in prison, the culture of silence is so overwhelming that few have had the courage to do so.

Any woman entering prison in Britain has two major problems to contend with. The first is the 'outside' life over which she loses control from the minute she begins her sentence. Who will care for the children? If they go into care, will she ever get them back? What about her home? Will it be broken into and her possessions stolen? Who will pay the rent? Will she lose her job? The second is survival in a hostile environment. New rules of behaviour must be learnt, both to comply with the expectations of those in authority, and in order to be accepted by other prisoners. There is the shock, too, of experiencing for the first time some of the most inhumane aspects of prison life: the lack of privacy; primitive sanitation (many prisons do not have toilets in the cells and women have to use a bucket or potty); long hours confined in a small space; poor food; frequent strip searches (a practice all women find humiliating and degrading); the loss of virtually all rights and the complete lack of power to make even basic decisions. The different ways in which women come to terms with these experiences are described vividly in the accounts which follow.

These problems affect all prisoners, regardless of gender, but we believe that in general women face more acute difficulties inside prison than men.

Because there are so few women's prisons, women are liable to be imprisoned much further from home than men. Prison rules and long and expensive journeys limit the amount of contact a prisoner may have with the friends and family whom she must rely upon to sort out personal affairs whilst she is inside. This reliance on others inevitably causes frustration and stress, and many women, of course, have no friends or family to help in this way.

Over half of all women sent to prison have dependent children. Most are cared for by relatives, but if there is no one who can look after them whilst their mother is inside, they are taken into the care of the local authority. That can be the start of a vicious spiral from which there is no easy escape. For example, if a woman's sentence is longer than a year she is likely to lose the tenancy of any home she may have occupied and, without any-where to live on release, she will find it impossible to take her children out of care.

Racism is also a major concern for women in prison. Many of the staff are racist in their attitudes and language. Few concessions are made for different dietary needs or particular hair and skincare products required. Recognition of and facilities for the practice of certain religions are also inadequate. Only recently have race relations officers been appointed within the prison system. They receive two weeks training and are monitored internally by the Home Office.

Other minority groups also suffer, particularly those with disabling physical or psychological conditions. Women who suffer from phobias, diabetes, epilepsy, asthma, or from poor sight or hearing are all treated with suspicion and little sympathy. Lesbians too are frequently vilified, and prison staff can be homophobic to the point of cruelty. Sexual relationships are not allowed, and even the casual linking of arms and affectionate embraces are not tolerated. Women are thus denied essential comfort and support. Many of these points, and the injustice and pain that they cause, are illustrated clearly in the accounts that follow.

The day-to-day life of women in prison is boring, monotonous and unproductive. Staff shortages can result in women spending twenty-three or even twenty-four hours a day locked in their cells, and when they are able to go to 'work' they must do only menial tasks – endless cleaning and washing of already clean floors on hands and knees, machine-sewing prison shirts and army uniforms, or mundane factory-type work.

The opportunities for education are often limited, making the acquisition of qualifications and degrees extremely difficult, if not impossible. For example, in Durham, the maximum-security wing for women, those who want to study have to do so in the evenings after the workroom has closed. Moreover, educational facilities and courses offered vary from one prison to another. If a woman is able to study for a particular examination in one prison, there is no guarantee that she will be able to continue if moved to a different institution.

All prisoners earn a prison wage, which for women is currently around £2.20 a week. This enables them to buy a few items (at outside prices) such as shampoo, toothpaste, tobacco and stamps in the canteen, or prison shop. The amount of tobacco that can be bought is so limited that it is always a valuable bargaining commodity. Those who smoke heavily are reduced to the humiliating practice of picking butts from the floor and the officers' rubbish bins. Women prisoners, unlike men, wear their own clothes, although they are limited to three sets of clothing and two pairs of shoes. The lending of any item, including clothing, is a punishable offence. The use of cosmetics is also severely restricted; items such as perfumes, lotions, eyebrow tweezers and razors are forbidden.

Most of us probably carry a mental image of prisons as being full of convicted offenders or 'criminals' serving out their 'punishment'. The truth is very different. Many of the women are on remand, waiting either to go on trial or for their sentence.

Remand in custody is the period during which prisoners experience prison for the first time. **Unconvicted remand prisoners** are held in prison while waiting for trial. Throughout this time, despite the legal presumption of innocence, they must conform to the normal prison regime. No concessions are made, apart from a few extra 'privileges' including the possibility of a daily visit lasting not more than fifteen minutes. Visitors to unconvicted remand prisoners may bring in a small amount of food, drink and tobacco. Even for those who live near the prison, such a brief visit is hopelessly unsatisfactory. But for women from, say, the Midlands held on remand at Holloway, or those at Durham's Low Newton who come from Cumbria, these provisions are totally inadequate.

Convicted remand prisoners are those who have pleaded or been found guilty by the courts and are held in prison, often so that psychiatric or social inquiry reports can be prepared before sentence is passed. It is hard to imagine any situation in which it would be more difficult to prepare realistic psychiatric or social assessments than in the distressing and isolating surroundings of a prison. Convicted remand prisoners are not entitled to daily visits and are, to all intents and purposes, treated like sentenced prisoners. About two-thirds of women held on convicted remand eventually receive a non-custodial sentence.

Once sentenced, women in England and Wales are usually sent to Holloway, Pucklechurch, Low Newton, New Hall or

Risley – whichever is the nearest – in the first instance. From there, depending on their age, length of sentence and perceived security risk, they are sent to the prison where they will serve the longest part of their sentence. For example, the majority of women life-sentence prisoners, and those considered a high security risk, are sent initially to Durham. In Scotland, Cornton Vale serves the functions of remand prison, youth custody centre and prison for convicted adult women, including Category A women prisoners, so all women remain there throughout their sentences.

In England and Wales women who give birth while in prison or who have a young baby when they are sentenced may be placed in one of the three **mother and baby units** which exist at Holloway, Styal and Askham Grange. These units provide a total of thirty-four places, with a further forty places for pregnant women. At Holloway and Styal (both closed prisons) babies may remain with their mothers until they are nine months old; at Askham Grange (an open prison) they are allowed to stay until they are eighteen months old. These age limits are quite rigidly adhered to, and take no account of the possibility of the mother's being released early on parole. In Scotland's Cornton Vale, each house has facilities for one mother and baby, though it seems that very few women choose to keep their babies there with them. If a woman is not due for release until the baby is beyond the age limit, or if it is felt by the prison and social services that she will be unable to care for her baby after release, then mother and baby are separated before the baby is four weeks old. This assessment is undertaken by prison officers and nurses who watch the mother in the restrictive environment of the mother and baby unit. Other factors such as whether her other children are in care are also taken into account.

These units have attracted a great deal of criticism both from women who have been through them and from those working in the field of ante-natal care and childcare. They argue that the standard of care compares badly with that outside; that the staff are in some cases insufficiently trained, and that many have outmoded views on childcare. The lives of the mothers and babies are regimented according to the prison programme, so that women who are expected to work or attend classes for at least four hours a day find it impossible to breastfeed on demand. There is little understanding or acknowledgement of cultural differences in childrearing, either: for example, women are not allowed to carry their babies in slings. Taking the baby into bed to feed or comfort her is a punishable offence.

Medical attention for all women in prison is provided by the Prison Medical Service, which is entirely separate from the National Health Service. The rate of sickness amongst women is very high: according to the Annual Report of the Prison Department for 1985–86, over 25 per cent in 1984–85 reported sick on any one day. Many prisons have a full-time medical officer, but those without this facility have contracts with a local GP who will attend the prison. Convicted prisoners have no choice as to which doctor they see and have no right to a second opinion. Specialist attention is provided by consultants who attend the prison, but whilst working there they are under contract to the Prison Medical Service. Prisoners are taken to NHS hospitals only for emergency treatment, surgery and to give birth, and are usually accompanied by a uniformed officer who remains with them throughout.

The level of prescription of psychotropic drugs to women prisoners is high. Although many women entering prison are already taking large doses of tranquillisers, they are given little or no help in cutting down. The widespread use of psychotropic drugs in women's prisons is clearly shown in figures available in the Prison Department Annual Report. For example, the total dosage of psychotropic drugs administered per head in 1983 ranged from 247 in Holloway and 295 in Cookham Wood and Styal, to 39 in Pentonville (a men's prison in London). Some prisoners maintain that psychotropic drugs or the 'liquid cosh' are used as a means of control. Those who are addicted to hard drugs such as heroin or cocaine get no treatment at all. The only drug therapeutic unit for women in prison (in Holloway) was recently closed down.

One of the most destructive aspects of prison life is the lack of contact with family and friends. Although the prison rules state that 'special attention shall be paid to the maintenance of such relations between a prisoner and his (sic) family as are described in the best interests of both', the women's own testimony reveals that this special attention is seldom given.

Sentenced women and girls are entitled to one half-hour visit every twenty-eight days. Although many prisons allow two visits in twenty-eight days, sometimes for longer than half an hour, these 'privileges' are entirely at the discretion of the prison governor and officers. The DHSS will pay travelling expenses for close relatives on benefits or very low incomes once every twenty-eight days. Partners other than husbands or common-law husbands cannot claim travel expenses, thus discriminating against lesbians. Meetings usually take place in communal visiting rooms closely observed by prison staff, whose main concern is that contraband should not be passed during the visit. Such security inevitably takes precedence over the need for privacy and inhibits physical contact, even with children. Women in some prisons, and particularly in Durham H Wing, are regularly strip searched after a visit, and their visitors may also be searched before a meeting.

Few prisons provide a play area for children, and some do not even have toys in the visitors' area or facilities for buying refreshments. Even where play facilities are provided, women prisoners have to remain at the table and are not allowed to join in their children's games. A child may sit on her mother's knee only with permission, granted at the discretion of the officers on duty.

Unlike women prisoners in many other countries, women in closed prisons in Britain do not have use of a telephone. All personal letters to and from women in prison (other than in the three open prisons) are censored by the prison officers. They are read and checked for contraband. Letters written in languages other than English are sent to approved translators and can be delayed for weeks. The knowledge that letters will be read inhibits many people from expressing themselves fully. This in turn can lead to misunderstandings and tensions between the women and their families and friends, thereby jeopardising the only links the women have with the world outside.

Maintaining 'good order and discipline' is the central theme of prison life. As the accounts by the women in this book illustrate so clearly, a myriad of rules and standing orders governs everyday life. Women are frequently not given the standard prison information book (written only in English), which includes a list of the basic offences against prison discipline, when they enter prison. The prison rules are generally available in the prison library but few women ask for them in case they are seen by the staff as 'troublemakers'. Those who do not speak English or who can neither read nor write may serve their sentences in complete ignorance of the prison rules and of what constitutes an offence against discipline.

Women prisoners are disciplined more than twice as often as men. In 1986, 3.6 offences were punished per head of the female prison population, as against 1.6 per head of the male prison population. A much higher proportion of prison rule offences committed by women fall into the 'mutiny or violence' category than by men, which is surprising given that all the major prison riots have occurred in men's prisons. It is impossible to tell from statistics whether women behave more disruptively in prison, whether the offences that women are being punished for are as serious, or whether the rules are more rigidly imposed in women's prisons. The second interpretation is widely accepted and would imply that women are likely to be disciplined for behaviour which would be tolerated in men's prisons.

The Prison Disciplinary System exists to adjudicate and punish those accused of committing any offence under the prison rules. There are twenty-one different 'offences'. Charges range from doing 'gross personal violence to an officer' through 'using foul and abusive language' to the catch-all 'offending against good order and discipline'. This vague wording can all too easily be interpreted as doing anything the prison officer on duty does not like. The prison governor (or other governor grade) adjudicates in cases where the charges are less serious. More serious matters are currently heard by members of the Board of Visitors (BOV; see below). Before the hearing, the

the prisoner has to be found fit for adjudication and punishment by the medical officer, for she may be confined to her cell and solitary confinement for long, highly stressful periods. It is almost unheard of for a doctor to find someone unfit for punishment. A visit to the psychiatric unit at Holloway in 1985 by H.M. Inspectorate of Prisons found that of a random sample of forty women found fit by doctors for adjudication, thirty-two had a wide range of conditions including brain damage and mental impairment.

Punishment for offences against discipline can be loss of remission, cellular confinement (including time in the punishment block), or withdrawal of 'privileges' – that is, no tobacco, no association and no radio. Offences which contravene the criminal law as well as the prison rules can be referred to the police and heard in outside courts in the usual way. Internal adjudications, whether conducted by the governor or BOV, broadly follow the pattern of court hearings, except that the prisoner must represent herself at governors' hearings and has no right to legal representation at BOV hearings – requests for representation are often turned down. Prisoners can call witnesses in their defence, but again the Governor or BOV may decide not to hear their evidence. All too often cases come down to a prisoner's word against an officer's. It is unrealistic to expect that managerial considerations such as the need to support staff are ignored when those sitting in judgment decide whose version to believe.

The Board of Visitors is a group of local magistrates and lay people appointed to each prison by the Home Office. They have a dual function: as the local 'watchdogs' ensuring adequate conditions and proper treatment of prisoners, and as the 'higher tier' in the prison disciplinary system, sitting in judgment on prisoners who are alleged to have breached the prison rules. These two functions can often be in direct conflict, and it is hardly surprising that most prisoners consider these 'watchdogs' toothless and have little faith in the ability or willingness of BOVs to intervene on their behalf if they wish to complain about some aspect of prison life. BOVs also produce an annual report for the Home Secretary on 'their' prison. These reports are not normally published.

Women's prisons are dangerous and unhealthy places. They are chronically overcrowded and the risk of fire is everpresent. Although an inordinate amount of cleaning takes place every day, prisons are notoriously unhygienic and frequently infested with cockroaches, fleas and mice. Local authority health and fire inspectors have no power to inspect prisons, which are still protected by Crown immunity. Prisons are criticised year after year by H.M. Prison Inspectorate for their lack of fire precautions and insanitary conditions. Yet nothing is done.

The accounts that follow speak of intense anguish, sorrow, frustration and anger. They also convey courage, solidarity and humour and a clear understanding that the system which deals with women in prison is degrading, inhuman and fundamentally flawed.

Martia

Martia was aged twenty-two at the time we spoke to her and had two children: Sasha, sixteen months and Tanya, two months. She had spent a total of twenty-two months in prison for a series of different offences, mainly theft and 'dipping' (pickpocketing). She had been living in a hostel for women in North London for the past year and was waiting to be re-housed.

The first time I went to prison I was nineteen. It was a forgery charge – cheques. I left home in Birmingham when I was fourteen. From then on I've just been going around from city to city causing trouble, more or less. I didn't get on too well at home. There was three of us – the twins Angela and Lorraine, and me. We are not from the same father and there was always that ice which never was broken. The atmosphere was really bad. Things didn't go right in the house so I left and ran away. Time and time again I went back, but one day, I said, 'Right I've had enough.' I was fifteen when I actually left home for good.

When I was sixteen I was put in a home for bad children. I ran away from that and went to Glasgow, caused trouble down there. I was wanted so I ran away again and came down to London. I met this guy named Desmond. I was really goody-goody until I met him! He got me into pickpocketing, doing cheques and all them kind of things. I was living with Desmond and I used to have to give him every goddamn penny.

Well, one day I got arrested. I just couldn't get away from the police. I gave them false names, they checked my fingerprints and found out who I was. I went to court and got nine months. I had been in trouble before, but then I'd been given probation and community work. This one was for £500 cheque fraud. That wasn't counting what I had in my pockets when I was arrested. I was just greedy, you see. I never used to go in the shops, I used to go in the banks. [Most shops won't accept a cheque for goods costing more than £50. A food processor costing, say, £48 will not fetch more than £35 on resale. Although the transaction is a great deal riskier, a bank will pay out £50 with a £50 cheque card.]

I was in Holloway on remand when I got my sentence. I was there for another month, then they sent me to Bullwood Hall. That was easy compared to Holloway. I didn't have too many hassles. But the time I done in Holloway really turned my head. When I first arrived I felt lost, I was wary of everything. I just kept my mouth shut and watched what was going on. I was really, really frightened – more of the girls than of anything else. My idea of prison was that it was somewhere where you were locked up and picked on all the time – that was my impression. I knew people who had been to prison and they told me, 'It's really bad in there, it's hard. They'll crack you up, you know, you feel like killing yourself.' All them kind of things. In fact, the reception was the worst, when they stripped me. I didn't know what to do. I kept thinking to myself, 'They're going to rape me now.'

For the first three sentences I done, I was still with Desmond. He never got sent to prison. I done his bird for him: I think it's what you call love or something! I wasn't scared of him, he was only a skinny little thing; I suppose I must've loved him. He used to come and visit me all the time, he brought money and a radio and them kind of luxuries. They make a difference inside. It was the radio which used to keep me going in Holloway. Being Black wasn't a problem. Some of the girls were bitchy, some of them were National Front, some of them were skinheads, but you knew who to mix with and who not to mix with. The Black girls tended to stick together, but me, I mix with everyone, I don't care. Colour's got nothing to do with it as far as I'm concerned. But even I used to get a lot of hassle with the Black girls who'd go, 'Ooh, you white man lover, you pagan!' and all these kinds of things, and I'd go, 'Yes, I know that, I love it.'

I had nowhere to go when I left Bullwood. I was of no fixed abode, but I'd finished my time so they still let me go. I gave them a bogus address but they didn't check it out. It never existed. I went back to Desmond and got myself into more trouble because as soon as I got out I wanted money. I went on the game this time and earned a bit of money there, and I did chequebooks and cards. It was Desmond who put me on the game – that lasted for a few months, then I got fed up with it. I just felt dirty all the time. I'm a professional chequebook girl and pickpocket. I think I was born to do that kind of thing, it's terrible. As for cards, I can clean them myself as well, and put my own signature on them, no problem. [Remove the original signature with solvent and replace it with the legitimate owner's name in her own handwriting. This makes forgery far less risky.] I used to duplicate chequebooks at times; I was thorough. But being out there loitering, that wasn't my line at all. Anyway, I left him. One night I was out making some money. I met this guy and made a grand, so I thought, 'Right, this is it. I'm going my own way now.' I haven't seen him since – well, not to talk to.

I lived in a squat in Battersea. I went out of a daytime working, chequebooks and all that kind of thing, but it gets boring after a while. Then I got arrested for some petty thing, shoplifting. It was Marks and Spencer. I tried to clean it out with a trolley. I filled it up and I was walking out the door as if nothing was happening and got arrested. I gave a fake name, they let me out on bail. Then I went out again, chequebooking in the West End, got arrested again and this time I got a six-month sentence. I done all of that one in Holloway.

I found that sentence easier because I knew what I was getting into. I knew what the score was, let's put it that way. From day one it was easier. But it's a dirty dump, it just depresses you. I reckon the prison staff are just as bad as the police, in their own way. Once you go through reception they don't know what you're like, or what your background is, but they tend to be rough with you and push you and see how far they can go – and most of the girls crack. In reception they put you in a little cubicle like a wardrobe and you have to sit there for hours. That second time I went in they left me there for two hours, and I was really cracking up. I had sweat all over my face and as soon as they opened the door I just went for one of them. I was taken down to the block [punishment wing] and they left me there for two days. They threw my meals in at me. The food went on the floor and everything. They do it to test people, to see how far they can push you. I crack at those kind of things. I get all frustrated. All you want is revenge. I don't know what anyone else says, you've only got to be in prison a week – no, a day – and all you want when you get out is revenge, to go and get drunk and do something really stupid like break a shop window or something. The anger inside fills up. It's the way they treat you. Some of them are fair, some of them treat you reasonably good, but others say you're just a criminal, a nothing, don't know what you were born for, that sort of thing. Impatience builds up and you just want to lash out and get them. I used to be quiet until I went to prison. Now I'm a loud-mouth, a bully, I retaliate to everything. That's what I had in my heart: revenge. I used to sit down and plan the day when they'd open the gate. I mean, you're just in a cell, you're locked up, it makes you think, 'Right, that was my mistake, but next time I'm going to get further, I'm going to get the better of them. When I get out there, I'm going to make sure I do something worthwhile – you know, like a robbery or something.' I was sitting in there planning robberies.

There should be something else, not prison. Prison hasn't solved my problems. If someone had sat me down when I was young and said, 'All right, tell us your problems,' I don't think I would have got into the trouble I did. I would have been a bit more calm, I would have thought, 'There's someone out there who cares.' My family have all gone to America now; left me and my kids in England. I've got no one else. They packed their bags, sold the house and left me: I got that news in prison. I mean, if someone's in prison, they shouldn't tell people news like that. I want to know that someone out there cares for me, not that I've got no one or nothing. I'd been in there four months and they came and told me they'd gone to America. I said, 'How do you know?' They said that they left a message with my solicitor and I just cracked. It was so bad. Instead of getting someone to calm me down and talk to me, a whole bunch of them came and jumped on me and rushed me down to the block and left me there. No one to talk to me or nothing. I asked for a priest. They said, 'Yeah we'll get one.' I still haven't seen the priest to this day. I was so unhappy. That made me just want revenge. On everything and everybody. I didn't care about nobody. I had nothing to lose. So as soon as I was released from prison I done more crimes. I went back in and out again, done more crimes and back in again. I was always wanted for something, and I was never in one place for too long. I didn't sign on or claim money or nothing, so I had to go out there and steal to get money in my pocket and clothes on my back. I wasn't interested in education or any sort of training. When I was in Holloway I used to go to education but that was just to get out of my cell. I wasn't interested in anything, I just didn't care. It was just me, it still is now, even though I've got kids. It's just me against that big thing out there. It's very hard, I tell you. There's times I want to talk to someone who belongs to me. There's nobody there. If it wasn't for the kids, I'd probably be out there now doing something silly. Prisons aren't good for no one. People come out and commit more crimes. Tension just builds up and it builds up, and when you come out you say, 'Right, I've got nothing to lose anyway, I've been to prison so I know what it's like. So what?'

When I went to Drake Hall on one sentence I was waiting for another court case as well, a conspiracy case, a big one. The conspiracy was to defraud giro cheques. That was me and Desmond, we duplicated them and he printed them out for something like £150 each. I knew I would get a big sentence. I thought to myself, 'I'll go mad in that prison. I'm not ready to go there yet. I want to see a little bit of life.' So I just took off. I'd been in Drake Hall a week. They've got this book which you have to sign in the morning. I signed myself in and then I just went. I ran through the fields, laid low for about two hours, then I made my way to the motorway and hitched it to Birmingham. I took a wallet from Birmingham New Street Station and got a train to London. I knew where I was going. I'd planned it all out, not the day, just got up one morning and thought, 'This is it, I've had enough. I'm going.' I'd nothing to lose. D'you know what I mean? I'd no responsibilities, no home. I just wanted to get out and live my life. If they catch me, they catch me. It's a chance I took. I felt good when I woke up in the morning and I thought, 'Yeah this is it, I'm going.'

I was out for four and a half months, then I gave myself up because I was carrying my daughter, Sasha. You can't run with a baby, and I'm not going to drag my kids into the sort of life I've been living. They sent me to Holloway and then to Styal. I came out just before the baby was born.

Prison is much better when you're pregnant. The problems of being in prison and getting out of prison are still there, but it's easier. Everyone says like, 'Leave her alone because she's pregnant', or you can get off some of the work. You still have to do scrubbing and cleaning, though. And the medical treatment in Holloway wasn't very good. In Holloway they don't take you out to the ante-natal clinic or get you a scan or nothing; Styal they do. All you get in Holloway is vitamin tablets or iron tablets. You had to be on your deathbed before someone would come and see you. There was one pregnant girl in there, we knew she was losing her baby. We told them she was losing the baby, but they thought it was just a scam for her to get out of the cell. We were saying, 'The girl is bleeding', but no one would listen and she lost the baby. She was about three months gone. It caused a lot of tension, riots, and they barricaded the cells. There was fights and lots of trouble.

Holloway mother and baby unit is disgusting. You get virtually no fresh air, nothing, you're just in the cells. There was eight girls, all pregnant, all locked up in one big dormitory, smoking. You can't tell a girl not to smoke a roll-up; they need their smoke. Everyone was getting on each other's nerves, and there was tension all the time. We only got off the unit for exercise about twice a week. There was times when people were saying nothing to nobody. It used to crack me up. I just used to read. I never used to be able to read good before I went into prison: I used to get into the book and think, 'What's that word?' and then cut the word down to size until I made up what it was. My reading's brilliant now.

The food was terrible. Best was Styal; Holloway food was always cold. I lost so much weight in there, although most of it was down to worry, stress: 'My baby's going to come out this and that.' Funny things go through your mind when you're pregnant. In prison they get worse. We had fifteen minutes association a day – or sometimes just three times a week. All we did was go down the corridor, nothing whatsoever to do. Some girls used to knit, the Africans would do people's hair, but that was it. It was so blooming depressing. I used to stand by the window and look out. Boredom, boredom, boredom. It was so bad.

Styal was much better. Every night you had association, every day exercise. At Christmas some of the girls nicked some apples and made apple wine. The staff knew what was going on but they turned a blind eye. I was on Fox House, then on Mellanby. Fox is for all pregnant women and Mellanby for women over six months pregnant and mothers and babies. We used to go out every two weeks for ante-natal checks and mix with the people. When they seen us they knew we'd come from the prison and used to sit back and grab their handbags sort of thing. Two officers came with us. Some of them used to wear normal clothes if they were going home afterwards, some would come in uniform but without their keys. But people just knew. We were coming in, white, black, Indian, they knew exactly what was going on. The nurses and doctors were lovely.

All my best laughs have been in prison. Sometimes when we

were feeling low someone might say, 'I've had a visit, look what I've got,' sort of thing, and we'd all have a nice time. We're in prison – so what? It's no big thing. They can't keep us here for ever, one day we'll get out and then we'll let them know about it. I'm a big-mouth person, I love trouble. If I'm not getting what I'm supposed to, I'll start. Oh I'll start. I always stand up for myself. I wouldn't take no shit from nobody. 'Screws, I don't care what you are, just leave me alone. I want to do my bird and get out' sort of attitude. Some of the staff were wary of me. Some of them said, 'We've met worse than you, you're nothing.' I suppose I didn't get in too much trouble in prison though. I was mouthy but that was about it. I only got into a couple of fights.

After I left Styal I came here. Sasha is sixteen months, and Tanya is two months. I had them both here. If it weren't for my kids now I'd be doing untold things. I'm a thinker and when I think everything is bottled up and tension comes, I just want to lash out. Even this house is like prison sometimes. You see what happens here, people just don't seem to care. They're just out of prison and they want to get high all the time and enjoy themselves. But you can't do that all the time. You've got to come down to reality and plan out your life, look at where you're coming from and where you're going. No one seems to want to do that. They just want to stay on cloud nine. Me and a girl had a fight last night. I really regret it now, but at the time everything was right up to there, you know. I thought, 'I'm going to burst, I know I'm going to burst.' I came upstairs and shut my door, and then the door went 'Bang, bang' and the kids woke up – this was one o'clock in the morning – and I go, 'That's it', went down and there was this big fight. I can take so much. When I was in prison I used to grip my fingers and bite my tongue and think, 'Right, don't do anything.' I used to have to go to the toilet if I thought I was going to fight anyone, or just go to bed and close my eyes and think, 'Not long, not long, not long to go', to keep myself down there.

I don't know what the point of prison is. I think it's to make us realise that you get punished for what you do, but it doesn't work like that. You don't get treated right. How can I put it? They don't do the right things. If they want to punish us, right, punish us, but don't torture us, get it over and done with. Don't just prolong the issue, don't pick on us and lock us in a room thinking that when we come out we're going to be as good as gold, because we're not. In that space of time you're going to build up hatred. All you want is vengeance. Another thing is, in prison you mix with everyone, and I think that made me worse as well. The people who had more experience used to teach me lots of things. I always wanted to get out and practise, to see how far I could go. I just learnt some more badness in there.

To come somewhere like this would have been better, somewhere where I had to be in at a certain time, where I couldn't have certain people come in. That would have helped me more than going to prison and mixing with all them people and just getting depressed and fed up and full of hatred. I would have been a better person than I am today. I'm a nice person, but when I get going I'm like a madwoman. It's all from the prison. You realise that this world is not easy and you have to fight if you want to survive in it, like all the way, non-stop. As soon as you stop you're going down. So I just keep going. If I have no money today I'm just going to go out and get some money for me and my kids. I'll not go without for no one, even if I go to prison for life. Nobody ever gave me a chance. If I'd had just one chance I wouldn't be where I am today.

Going back to my family now, I've always been the black one of the family. They used to call me Blackie sometimes. I was the darkest one. I didn't have a chance to prove that I'm somebody as well, that I'm not nothing. I'm a human being, with my own mind, my own thoughts, my own ideas. I've got a lot of resentment that needs to come out, not on my kids nor on me, or on anybody. It needs to come out and go away. Sometimes I get so frustrated, I say to someone, 'Listen, just take the kids. I have to go out or else I'm going to crack.' There are days when I sit down and my mind goes back to prison, when I'd be looking out the window, thinking, I wish I was out there, you know, doing something.

I haven't seen my family for three years, not since they left.

I mean, Angela, one of the twins, we used to be close. I think she understood me, probably more than anyone else, more than my mum. Then me mum went to America and took Angela with her, left no address or nothing, and so it's just me – no father, no nothing. I can't tell you how lonely it feels, it really does. I just feel, 'God, hurry up and grow up, kids, and talk to me and be my friend.' If only I had someone to talk to. I feel lost sometimes, like I ain't got no one.

I think people who go to prison must have had a reason for whatever they did. It may not be a good reason to us, but they must have had a good reason to do it, either family-wise or tension-wise, or because of life in general. Some people like prison because they make more friends in there. I've been going for so long I can do everything. I never refuse help, don't get me wrong, but not all the time. Sometimes I just want to be left alone to do it my way, whether it's right or wrong. It's just bloody, life is a rotten thing, just horrible. Through all my sentences, and if you add them together, I've done twenty-one, twenty-two months in all, there's never been one day when I've kept my mouth shut, without an argument or something. The tension's there and it comes out in bits and bobs, either on one of the girls or one of the staff. Being told to do things like not run in the corridor, or stand up when the governor comes in. I never used to stand up. 'Why should I stand up to you? Who are you, you're not the Queen', and I used to sit down, get pulled up by the girls: 'Come on.' 'No why should I stand up? They can't do nothing worse to me, I'm already locked up. What else can they do? Put me down the block? So what? I'll be out in two days, I don't care.'

Holloway is the worst prison. It deserves to be closed down. I mean C1 [the psychiatric unit] is the worst. We used to pass sweets and things to some of the girls down there if we passed the windows. You can hear them screaming and banging their heads, crying that they want to go home. You felt it, you really felt it. I was in a wing just above it. At night I used to put the pillow on my head and just hold it so as I couldn't hear. If you're not really strong in your mind and find things to occupy yourself you can go mad in there, get taken down to C1 and then to the madhouse.

In the block they put you in a gown – a strip dress, no knickers or bra, and your clothes and shoes outside the door. Then they just leave you. No furniture, just one chair and a mattress on the floor, and nothing to do at all. It was dirty and smelly and you used to get spiders and cockroaches: it makes me feel 'ergh' just to think about it. Sometimes they'd forget about you and just leave you down there. It used to be for really petty things like not standing up, or shouting out the window, running up the dinner queue and pushing it. Petty things like that. One girl had a fight and she was down there for weeks. We did a protest to get her up again. There was going to be a riot so they brought her up. Prison's not the right place for most people. Some find that they get better treated in there than they do outside, but for the others it's just rubbish. Some officers think it's their duty to go around, you know, 'Right, we've got the keys and you ain't going nowhere.' They're not that good themselves. I could tell you some things about them!

I like fancy living. I like nice things and good things for my kids. I just have to have them. I knew that from day one, and wouldn't take the trouble of working and saving for them. I'd just go out there and get what I wanted. When you've got good clothes and things you feel better. You have more power, you feel more confident, and people don't look down on you. Of course I'll be out there doing my chequebooks again. It's so bloody easy. Only my present boyfriend stops me. I wanted to go out last week, but he said, 'No way, you're not going out there', and he made me stay in the whole week. I'm greedy. Once I get on to a good thing I keep it going until I run out of luck. I either come out on top or I get unstuck and get caught.

I have to find something to do to keep me out of trouble. I'd like to be a community worker, something like that – a social worker. Like in here everyone who has problems comes to me. I've put a note on my door saying, 'If you've got problems, please don't come today because I'm not in the mood.' Sometimes, three o'clock in the morning: knock, knock, knock –

'Martia, do you know what's happened?' But no one listens to my problems. It's not as if I haven't got any. Like right now I'm feeling lonely. I just wish my mum was here, someone who belongs to me. I wish I could contact her. If I had an address I'd be happier, I'd write to them and they'd write to me. I don't know where they are. No relations, nothing. It's hard. One day perhaps we'll all meet up. I hope it's not too late. I believe I hurt them when I ran away, and with my way of life. But I've come down a bit now. I've got more patience than I used to have, and now I've got responsibilities with the kids. I've just got to wait my time and think, 'Well, my day will come.' My nerves are no good no more. They used to be brilliant. I'm always shaking. I know I've only got to make one mistake and I'll go straight back in. My record's as long as my arm – even longer.

Still, if I thought my difficulties were bad enough, some have had it worse than me. Sometimes I'd sit down and look at somebody and hear their problems and think, 'I'm lucky. She don't know where she's coming from or where she's going.' I may have no one, but I know where I'm going in life, I've got a goal. I'm strong in mind, too, though it's only since the kids that I've got more patient and confident. Some good things might come out of me now. Sometimes when I'm in a mood I do untold things, I just pick on people. It's not fair, I haven't come off that ladder yet. But in many ways I think I'm okay. I've produced two lovely girls, maybe someday I'll be able to give them what they want. I won't leave my kids without a bloody good fight. I don't want them doing what I've done. I think there's someone else in me which I haven't given a chance to get out. I always used to go round mouthing to everyone: 'Who are you looking at, you white bitch and you black cow' and things like that. But that's not really me, because I can't defend it. I'd just like to get off my ladder and stop pretending to be somebody else, just be ordinary and not get away with doing this or that – and get away with it laughing. I'm not that kind of person. It's a relief, because now I can just be myself. People can look at me and talk to me. I even changed my name. Everyone used to know me as Sheena Rawlinson, but now I've got my name back: Martia

Miller. Maybe in some ways prison has helped me, but it's still not the answer.

When I came out of prison, I was wary. I wasn't scared, I was ready for anything. Now I've got a flat that I'll be moving in to soon. I feel really good about it. I'm on my own. I'm well scared. But mind over matter, I can do it if I really want to, and I will. If only for them I'll do it. This place has given me my first identity really. I've always been doing what this man told me or that man told me; now I'm doing things for myself. It feels good. It feels really good. When I first came to this room, I didn't like it, then I thought, 'Well at least it's mine. I've got the key to it, nobody else has' and I felt good.

I'm ready for life. I want to get somewhere, I don't want to be a crook or thief all my life.

Martia was arrested for assault three months after this interview and was held in custody for several weeks until she was granted bail. The children were put temporarily into the care of the local authority. At her trial she pleaded guilty, and was given a two-year prison sentence suspended for two years. If she is arrested for anything, however trivial, during that time, she is likely to have to serve two years in prison plus whatever sentence her new offence would attract. She has since married and is living in South London with her husband and her two children.

Janet

*Janet was thirty-one when she was arrested for possession of drugs.
She was sentenced to two years in prison. A single parent, she lived
with her daughter Karen, then aged ten, with whom she had a
particularly close relationship. Janet has suffered various forms of ill
health throughout most of her life, including asthma and a serious
thyroid deficiency.*

I was sentenced to two years in prison. My charge was supplying
cocaine and I was given two years for that and one year each
concurrent for possession of small amounts of cannabis, cannabis resin, amphetamines and LSD. I think they wanted to
make an example of me. The fact that I had people to speak for
me at the trial and that I was doing community work didn't
appear to mean much to them. I think the judge's mind had
been made up before I even stepped into the dock. It was almost
as if he was doing me a favour by not sentencing me for more,
even though it was only one specimen charge of supplying.
There was no 'intent to supply' or anything like that. I had two
previous charges of possession in '78, which technically should
have been spent. I had a conditional discharge for one and an
absolute discharge for the other. They were brought up in court
and I think that influenced his decision. I had been dealing in
coke to a very small circle of friends, not more than half a dozen.
It wasn't really dealing; it was an arrangement whereby being a
single parent on supplementary benefit I was able to get a little
for myself. I made very little money, just enough to run my car.

I've supplied dope since I was fifteen because I've never had any money. I wasn't dependent on coke, any more than it was nice to have a line after a heavy day – just like someone might have a glass of wine. It was certainly no more important to me and I could quite happily go for weeks without any. I only took it in social situations. It was like giving myself a little treat, like say buying a bottle of wine. I've never drunk, possibly because my mother, my grandmother and my daughter's father are heavy drinkers. I grew up with a thing about alcohol – I think that's got a lot to do with why I preferred a line of coke rather than a drink. I was able to take it or leave it.

My mother grassed me up, she went to the police. She searched my house and got information from my daughter, telling her that I was sick, that I needed help and that she wouldn't go to the police. My mother obviously found something in the house. She'd been trying to prove that I was on drugs since I was fourteen. The expression 'on drugs' turns my stomach. I had never presented myself like that to anybody. I had such a horrific adolescence and childhood, it's not surprising I found a way out, an escape from the pain. I was getting through by starting to smoke dope and take acid. I had no self-confidence at all until I was twenty-five. I had some very, very difficult years because of my childhood and adolescence. I am positive the only reason I'm still here is because I *did* take drugs. I found it impossible to make relationships, I was one hell of a mess. I had two nervous breakdowns when I was a teenager. Dope was my only means of escape. If it hadn't been dope it would have been valium: what's the difference?

My mother sat my daughter down and said something like, 'Look, I know your mother's up to something, she's sick, she needs help, we've got to help her. You tell me.' My daughter was then ten and a half. What an awful thing to do to her. I'm confident enough in my ability as a mother to know my daughter had never been pressurised by knowing there was a part of my life that was illegal. She'd grown up knowing that. She also knew that it meant that we could have a car when otherwise we couldn't. She had always been completely sensible and completely cool about it. There has been a close bond between us all her life. We grew up together, I've looked after her by myself from when she was two, which was when I split up from her father. I could always tell if she was under pressure, and she was always able to talk to me. I am absolutely convinced that if she was at all worried about my 'drug activities' it would have manifested itself, like in difficulties at school or something. One thing that I did tell her was that if I ever got arrested she would not be involved. That was another reason why I feel I let her down so much. My mother was always very jealous of the close relationship that my daughter and I had, and did all she could to come between us. I'm a pretty perceptive person, I understand people quite well, but I never dreamt that my mother could do anything that would damage my daughter so greatly.

She did it because she wanted to get custody of my daughter, that was her motive. She went to my daughter's school and told them, which resulted in my daughter's teacher making her a ward of court. My daughter was then in her last year at primary school. I had had nothing but glowing reports from her teacher. She'd always done very well, had lots of friends, been very settled, nothing to make me believe in any way that she was disturbed. My mother happened to see the woman who'd been my daughter's form teacher for the previous two years, who was known to interfere. In conversation with my mother it appears that she realised my mother was too unbalanced to have custody of my daughter, so therefore she made wardship proceedings herself. She didn't go to the Social Services or anything like that, she acted completely beyond the jurisdiction of any teacher. Her justification was that we were personal friends, which is absolute bullshit. I'd never even been to her house. Also I think it is very relevant that at this point my daughter's father was not involved. Nobody thought of asking him if he'd like custody. He'd been so disinterested in her progress during six years of primary school that he'd only ever visited the school once. You would have thought that the natural reaction of the teacher would have been that we ought to contact the father – better him than the nutty grandmother.

I was arrested on a Wednesday and kept overnight at the police station and questioned. The only reason the police got anything out of me was because they threatened to question my daughter. I didn't know that they could, but I'd always sworn to her that I would never involve her in any way and I've never broken my word. I would have admitted to murder to keep her out of it. I didn't know then that she had already been well questioned, by my mother, by her teacher, Uncle Tom Cobbleigh and all. She'd even been taken to the police station by the teacher to see if they, the police, wanted to speak to her. Luckily they hit on a nice policewoman who more or less had to throw the teacher out, she was so insistent and heavy. The teacher turned up at the police station at eight the next morning to tell me she was taking responsibility for my daughter. I said, thank you very much but I haven't even been charged yet, let alone convicted. I asked the police to ring her father and ask him to come and collect her from school. I was horrified to find out later that in fact he had not collected her from school but from the police station. I don't know what she was doing there. I can only think that the teacher wanted to get as much mileage from the whole thing as she could.

They held me one night on a holding charge because they had to analyse the pharmaceuticals. They charged me with possession of cannabis. I was then granted unconditional bail, in spite of the fact that the magistrates knew all about the cocaine, which was one of the reasons I thought I'd never get a sentence. I just had to sign on at the police station once a week – no surety, unopposed bail, no problem at all. I spent all the next seven months waiting for my case to come up and fighting to keep my daughter.

I wasn't corrupting anybody. I wasn't exactly selling drugs to teenagers: most of my friends were in the music business in London, and you can't find a business which goes more hand in hand with it. I didn't supply to anyone in my home town. I kept my two lives very separate. I was that content with being a mother I'd decided I didn't want a job until my daughter went to secondary school. I was offered this amazing job in London, but I felt no, I've got plenty of time, I'd rather be with her until she goes to secondary school. I was brought up by au pairs, there's no way I'd do that to my child. It was my responsibility I brought that child into the world, and there was no way I was going to thrust her off onto other people. I didn't see it as a choice between that and continuing an illegal existence. I saw it as a choice of what I believed to be my obligations, how I see motherhood.

Karen stayed with her father. I had to apply for access – access to my own daughter who I'd lived with all her life. We'd never been apart from each other for more than two weeks when I was arrested. I don't know how I coped with it. It was like a raving nightmare. I couldn't believe that it wouldn't resolve itself. I thought that someone would say, 'Hang on, this is all ridiculous. We know Karen, we know Janet, this is all mad.' My daughter's welfare seemed far more important, and it was really all I thought about. So I put very little energy into my criminal case partly because I didn't think I would go to prison, and certainly not for more than a month or two.

The police didn't want me to be sentenced, which I was stunned about. They seemed to be of the opinion that there should be a new form of charge for two levels of supplying, like what they call social supplying and big supplying. Technically, if you hand someone a joint you're supplying, but it means a lot of work for them and doesn't catch the people who are the big fish. And anyway, what you do among consenting adults is really your own business.

When I was sentenced I didn't even know what two years meant. I didn't know about parole. My doctor had also prepared a report for the judge, about various medical problems which I hoped might be taken into consideration, along with the fact that I had for some time been re-building my life and now had very little to do with the lifestyle that brought me into contact with drugs. I wasn't very happy with my legal representation; in fact, I think I could have done a better job myself. The whole thing seemed to be over with in five minutes – I'd hardly sat down before I was being taken down the steps to the police cells. It all seemed very unreal.

My solicitor and barrister came and saw me, and explained about parole and remission, and told me there was no point in appealing. I was absolutely stunned, I hardly knew what was going on. After a lot of pestering I was allowed to speak to two friends who had come to court with me, and I was appalled by having to speak to them through a glass and metal grille thing. I wasn't allowed to go anywhere near them at a time when I most needed reassuring. It was very frightening. A very young prison officer from Holloway was with me at the court. My solicitor's secretary had rung Holloway to find out what I was allowed to take, and was told three changes of clothes, flannel, books and basic things. I had taken very little, but this screw took great pleasure in going through all my things and saying I couldn't take most of it. When I got to Holloway I found I would have been entitled to take most of the things she wouldn't let me take, like a hairbrush. With hair as long as mine it's just impossible without one – I didn't have one for three weeks. I suppose that was my introduction to a totally dehumanising process. She seemed to get such delight in removing all those objects from me. I ended up with a couple of pairs of trousers, a couple of T-shirts, a jumper and a pair of shoes. After a fight, I was able to take three books. I was taken down to Holloway by car, with me on the back seat and her on one side and a male officer on the other side. I was very worried I was going to be sick.

The reception at Holloway was so confusing and everyone was so aggressive. I had to keep on signing bits of paper which were meant to list my property, but I had no opportunity to read anything. It was 'Sign this' and if you questioned anything you got shouted at. I'd taken a box of medication I was on at the time – drops I needed for my eyes, my asthma inhalant and things like that. This caused great consternation and a lot of mirth. They seemed to think I was a professional hypochondriac. I had a tremendous struggle to keep my medication the whole time I was in Holloway, and it started again when I went to Styal. I saw two nurses who also thought my medicines were very amusing. They thought I ought to see the doctor. Nobody seemed to accept that I'd been in charge of my own body and my own

31

medication for the best part of my life; they seemed to think that was a very strange idea. I saw the doctor who said I'd better go on the hospital wing, which seemed ludicrous simply because I needed to use eye drops and an asthma inhalant and asthma pills. I don't know whether it was because I was in there for drugs. I couldn't believe their attitude. I wasn't prepared for it. I was strip searched and told to have a bath. They did't make me wash my hair which I was very grateful for as I hate having to wash my hair in the bath. For three hours I was sitting in a dressing gown. I wasn't given anything to eat until six o'clock, I hadn't had anything all day.

The officer at the court had taken my jewellery off me. I'd left a couple of rings on which were really hard to get off. They eventually got them off me with baby oil, and almost took my fingers with them. It was so unnecessary; they weren't sharp or dangerous or big. They couldn't get my bracelet off. It became very important to me, like my only mark of identity. I'm very sentimental about my jewellery. I found having it taken away worse than the strip search. It really made me feel naked. The strip search seemed fairly pointless, inasmuch as they didn't go through my pockets. It would have been quite possible to put something into the pockets of my dressing gown and then put it back into my clothes when I took the dressing gown off.

Because I was going to the hospital wing I didn't get taken up until about nine o'clock, so I was the last one. All the other girls had gone and I was left by myself – no books, magazines or anything – wondering what was going to happen to me. They seemed to be making a point on reception of continually stressing, 'This is prison so you'd better get used to it.' There seemed to be an awful lot of officers making a tremendous noise, and they were all so heavy. They could see by my record that I hadn't been to prison before, didn't know the procedure. Nobody explained anything at all. You were expected by some telepathic way to know where to go, what to do. If you didn't, you were bawled out, and that took an awful lot of getting used to. It was really horrific.

When I finally got up onto the wing it was dark. I couldn't

believe how dirty it was. I thought prisons would be immaculate, and that in the hospital wing they'd be particularly fussy. It was really filthy. In the first cell they took me to, which was single, there was blood everywhere. That was the last straw as far as I was concerned. Then they decided perhaps I didn't have to stay in that one after all, so put me into another single cell, which was equally disgusting. There was a pile of really filthy-looking blankets on the bed, they got me some sheets and a towel, and I managed to get an extra pillow because of my asthma. There was a girl in the next cell who I was to see again later in Styal. She's very, very disturbed, and should never have been in prison. She screamed and screamed and screamed all night long. My first twenty-four hours in prison were difficult, very difficult.

The assistant governor [AG] who I saw four days after I got into prison told me I'd be going to Cookham Wood or Bullwood Hall in two to three weeks. I couldn't stay in Holloway because there wasn't room for sentenced women. There's only sixty places and they were all full. I'd also seen a probation person. He told me to try to go to Cookham Wood: in his words, 'There's a better class of prisoner there.' I didn't know any better. About eight o'clock on the eighth day I was told to pack my stuff up, because at seven o'clock the next morning I was going to Styal. I didn't even know where Styal was! When I found out I really kicked up. For a start, Styal had never been mentioned. I'd been hoping my daughter would be brought to see me at Holloway and was frightened of her turning up and finding me not there. I also knew I was very unlikely to get visitors as far away as Styal. Although Holloway was awful at least it was central and most of my friends were in London. Obviously, looking back, I'm overjoyed I only spent eight days there. The contrast between it and Styal couldn't be more marked.

Six of us went to Styal. The journey took ages. We were told we were going to stop at Coventry on the way for lunch. We all perked up. Nice one! We pulled into Coventry police station and instead of going to a café, as we had hoped, we got shut in one cell and left there for about two hours with the most revolting sandwiches you've ever seen in your life. It was a tiny cell, so we had to take it in turns to sit down. Three on a bench, three on the stone floor, usual cell toilet, no door on it or anything. All this came as such a shock. I must have been very naive. Like with the conditions at Holloway, I knew it would be no picnic, but I just didn't think they would treat human beings like that, anywhere.

We got to Styal mid-afternoon. Two of the women who were moved up with me had already been in prison, one for about a year, one for about eight months, so they knew what to expect. We were left in the waiting room for about three hours before anyone started dealing with us. We were just locked in, no food or anything. I finally got out of reception at around half-past seven, after going through the whole procedure, marking off all my stuff again (which was checked before leaving Holloway), and a strip search. Even though we'd come from another prison, we still had to be searched.

It was summer and Styal looked very attractive. The grounds are very nicely kept. From reception we could see girls walking around, although we were told by a very heavy officer that we were not to get any ideas that we could walk around freely. You had to have a reason for going from A to B, or else you were in trouble.

To my utter horror I was put on Fry House, which was the house for pregnant women at that time. The last thing I wanted when I was so worried about what was happening with my own daughter was to spend my sentence surrounded by pregnant women. When I got to the house, I found a far more relaxed atmosphere than at Holloway. I was amazed at the size of it, it felt vast, and I was put in a two-bedded room which I had to myself as the house wasn't full. It was really dilapidated and tacky. Again I was expecting military style spick and span. In the common room all the chairs were slashed and scratched, old curtains hung off their hooks, really dilapidated and depressing. No effort had been made to make it look homely at all. It seemed sad for the pregnant women, especially, to be in such a depressing house. The house officer was very young. I got to know her quite well eventually, very sort of 'jolly hockey sticks' and friendly. There was none of the constant supervision that you got in Holloway, just one officer on the house for twenty-two women, and no screw on at night, which absolutely amazed me. On the pregnants' house, though, a nurse stayed overnight, in case anyone went into labour. It was a lot friendlier and altogether more human than Holloway.

One officer, a really nice screw, a senior officer called Mrs [R], understood why I wanted to be moved off the pregnant house and got me moved the next day. I was moved to Martin, the most rowdy house in the prison. Whether that was down to the powers that be I don't know; perhaps they were teaching me a lesson for daring to complain about where I was put. Because I was older and a bit more staid I was going to have a hard time. Most of the women on Martin were Youth Custody trainees [YCs] and they could be a real pain. There was always girls in trouble and lots of fights and chaos. But you had to remember the circumstances they were there under – they should never have been there at all. It was age, youthful high spirits, they were very young, like puppies really. They were incredibly noisy and boisterous. No malice or anything. The YCs got punished more than anybody else and had a really hard time. Most of them went out and re-offended. I learnt very quickly that prison solved nothing. A very large proportion had been there before and would be there again.

You're allowed more things in Styal: one more set of clothes, more photographs, more books. But everything is so arbitrary; every screw interprets the rules differently, and there seems to be no rhyme or reason for anything. The first month this was very hard to understand. After you'd come to terms with everything and knew what was expected, life became easier. You had to learn each officer's quirks personally, because they not only interpreted the rules and regulations so very differently, they also made up their own as they went along. I spent a good while asking for something written down so that I could see what I was and wasn't supposed to do, but that was a forlorn hope. In fact it was treated as a joke. There's the green

Instructions for Prisoners book [information book], but it has virtually no relevance to anything to do with life in prison. I smuggled a copy out when I left because I thought it was so funny.

I had the same problem with the doctor and nurses in Styal over what I could and couldn't have in the way of eye drops, etc. Even though I'd eventually been allowed my inhaler and eye ointment in Holloway, it had all been taken off me again. The doctor's attitude was complete contempt. When I had my medical interview he said to me, 'You know what I think you should be in here for? Life.' Which was pretty heartening, considering it was down to him to do one of my parole reports and that most of the people in Styal were there for drugs, or drug-related crimes, like kiting cheques [passing stolen cheques] to buy drugs or shoplifting to buy drugs. Probably about 70 per cent of the women were in there because of drugs – a phenomenal proportion. It would have been much better if they had been getting some therapy to help them understand why they needed to take drugs in the first place. Some of them seemed to view it as a sort of health cure. They'd get a short sentence for shoplifting, clean themselves up, get out and then be in again within six months – young women.

Soon after your arrival you're interviewed and put on what's called 'house assessment' – house cleaning for the first five weeks – whilst the screws work out what would be the best work for you. You don't have much choice: cook (every house has its own cook), on the gardens, workroom, works, etc. Some jobs are more popular than others. The job that everyone considered bad was in the workroom, which was my absolute dread. I mean, I can't sew at all! It would have driven me mad to have been stuck behind a sewing machine all day, which some of my friends were. All the girls who were any sort of discipline problem and virtually all the older women ended up in the workroom. I felt bloody sorry for them. The money was good if you worked hard, really hard, but it took a while to get good enough on the machines to do that. The top wage in the prison was around £2.60 a week and £3 in the workroom, and the woman who ran it – a civilian instructor, not a screw – was a real old dragon who put people on report at the drop of a hat. You can easily lose a job or be moved as a sort of back-handed discipline. It's never proved or said that's why you lose a job, but it's a constant threat.

It was unusual if you got the job you wanted because that isn't how prison works. I was lucky, because instead of being on house assessment I was called and told I was going to be on the works party next day, only my second day at Styal. It caused a tremendous stink among the other women because that was a prized job, what's called a 'trusty's' job. Only those who they think are pretty responsible go on the works. I don't think anyone realised how strange it all was for me. I had only been in prison eight days. I still didn't know what was going on, and was still desperately worried about what was happening at home. Virtually everybody there had been held on remand or had been to prison before, so knew how the prison ran. I was pretty unusual in that respect. It transpired the reason why I was put on the works was because there was another woman on the works with the same surname who'd gone to Holloway for her appeal and they thought she'd come back and had got us mixed up.

I got on well. I enjoyed working with the outside tradesmen. It was a bit like being a general builder's apprentice. A number of men were employed to do up the houses one by one – they're slowly being modernised and decorated. You're apprenticed to a different tradesman each week, so no ties are formed. They were all over fifty at least. I should imagine it was a condition of employment: 'only geriatrics need apply!' I was very worried, because I had never done anything like it in my life and I'm not at all handy, but I got a reputation for being a worker. The best thing about it was the solitude. You're normally never alone in prison, especially being in a dorm with eight people, and if you're not used to it, the constant noise of people around you all the time is awful. My first day on the works I was sent off to whitewash a shed all by myself. It was bliss. Time passed by quite quickly. I worked really hard which meant I got tired and could sleep better at night. I didn't sleep for the first week in prison, I couldn't get used to the noise. I learnt how to paint a window properly, and tile a loo. There were twelve on the party, quite a small number. I got to know women from other houses. I was lucky I went straight into a trusty's job, and I could work at weekends as well, and I earned good money: £2.63 a week.

Every morning, even Saturday and Sunday, we were woken at seven. We had to be washed, dressed, have our hair immaculate (which was difficult because I had to plait mine), strip all the bedclothes off our beds (which seemed totally a pointless exercise and got right up my nose the entire time I was at Styal), and fold them to a complicated and immaculate design – sheet, blanket, sheet all wrapped round with the counterpane and put at the end of your bed. All that and down to sign the time book by 7.20. You had to queue to sign the book, as only one inmate was allowed in the office at a time. If you're late twice you're put on report, and girls often lost remission because of that. Twenty-two women, eight washbasins, two toilets, it's just impossible; twenty minutes to do all that and bunk your bed as well, and if you're sleeping in a bunk in a crowded room you're falling over each other trying to fold your sheets and blankets at the same time. I got it down to a fine art, but it was all additional pressure. Some screws were more lenient than others and you learned when you saw who came round to wake you up how much you had to hurry – whether it was one who'd put you on report if you were one minute late or if they would give you five minutes' grace. Some were really heavy.

Then you went into the common room, Radio One was put on, and breakfast was called at 7.30. Radio One was on all day, absolutely everywhere. It didn't bother me, but it used to bother some of the other women terribly, especially the older ones. You only had 20 minutes in the dining room and that included queuing up. Everyone used to fight to get to the front of the queue, as that way you usually got better portions. If you were last the food would be cold, because it all used to be laid out waiting for you to collect. Getting a hot meal was an art in itself! Breakfast was usually porridge, and Monday you got bacon, a big event: one half-starved rasher. You got your sugar ration in the morning which had to last all day: one egg cup full, a red plastic egg cup with ER on the bottom. It depended entirely on the screw as to how full they filled it; it could be anything from half-full to full. I soon learned to hide it because if you left it in the dining room or by your place somebody else would take it. Meals only used to take about five minutes to eat in there, everyone would eat really quickly. If you were near the front, it was nice to be able to have a roll-up and drink your tea slowly and wake up a bit. After breakfast you'd have until 8.25 to make your bed again, tidy your space and make sure it was absolutely immaculate.

You had to leave for work at 8.25. The house screws would stand out on the avenue to make sure that you didn't stop and talk. I worked from 8.30 to ten past twelve. We had a tea break which was only supposed to be for ten minutes, but the men took exception to this so we usually got a bit longer. Dinner was at 12.30. Before we left for dinner we had to be rubbed down [a body search], have our pockets checked, etc. All meals were in the house. How good the meal was depended entirely on what the cook was like, you couldn't believe the difference. Sometimes the food was totally inedible. If you were unfortunate enough to get a bad cook it took a while before the powers that be realised it, so you had to put up with inedible food for weeks. Sometimes it was completely burnt. We nearly always had milk pudding, rice pudding, semolina or some other stodge. I found that before long I was eating everything – most people did out of boredom. Also meals are an event, and measured out the days: the end of the morning, the end of the afternoon. You also got your mail at dinnertime, opened, read and censored by the screws during the morning. You went back to work at half-past one. We weren't allowed to go upstairs to our rooms without permission, that was a real blow for me. So we were all herded in the common room together. It was pretty small and there was never enough chairs for everybody. (A screw told me that a prison regulation stated that there should only be two chairs for every three women.)

On the works, I worked until ten to five which was a lot later than most other people, and this caused problems. Tea was at five and before tea you were meant to have changed out of your work clothes. If you didn't finish until ten minutes before, there was no way you could change and have a bath. Baths were something which caused continual problems. There were never enough to go around, especially on the house where I was, where there were two other girls on the works and four girls on the gardens all coming in filthy dirty and wanting a bath. There was always arguments. The screws eventually brought in a booking system but refused to put the bath book out until three o'clock. So if you happened to be out of the house working it was too bad, unless you got a house cleaner to put your name down for you.

Tea was at five, evening classes were at 5.50. I went to as many classes as I could, although as they worked college terms they didn't start until September and I arrived in July. Evenings without classes were dreadful. They really dragged just watching telly, and everyone wanted to watch the soap operas and sit coms. We had supper at eight which was usually a rock cake or a scone, or sometimes we had toast, and a cup of tea. We got coffee once a week. You had to be in bed and washed by nine o'clock at the latest; the house screw only left after she'd seen everyone in bed. If you were on a house that was causing problems, you got what was called babysitters, which meant two screws on the house all night. Howard, which was the 'muppet house' [house for women who were disturbed or particularly distressed], also had screws on all night. Then there were the screws they called night patrol. There were two sets of them. They went from house to house checking all night long. If you were caught out of bed or in bed with anyone else, you were instantly put on report. On Martin, where I was, someone would go to the washroom which looks over the pathways to act as lookout, so hardly anyone *did* stay in bed once the screw had gone off. The night patrol was meant to come and turn the lights off at a quarter to ten, but sometimes they wouldn't turn up until eleven or half eleven. They couldn't tell you off for not turning off the lights but you weren't meant to be out of your dorm or even out of bed. It was like reverting to childhood. When I was in the eight-bed dorm it was terribly noisy, but I just had to get used to it. Later on I managed to move to a quiet dorm which was really great and very essential to saving my sanity. In prison your whole level of tolerance to noise has to adjust.

A lot of the senior officers didn't like the houses being unattended. I heard before my release that they were thinking of having screws on the houses all night. I think that would be a great shame, especially for the younger ones. It was the only chance they had to let off any steam. It was difficult for the older people, they should have been a lot more thoughtful how they separated people for the houses. Not middle-class ghettos or anything like that, but simply by age. Every house had one or two people who were over forty-five and it was misery for them.

In prison you're always rushing and worrying. The first month was absolute hell, especially as I didn't have a watch. They'd shout 'Classes' and you might be in the bath! But you got used to it. You start to work like clockwork, doing it all automatically. From continually chasing my tail in the first month and being late for everything, and always being in trouble in varying degrees, punctuality became second nature. Once you knew what the routine was, it was much easier to fit in. It was dreadful while you couldn't remember what time tea break was, or what time breakfast was, or what time you were meant to line up for this, that or the other, or what time doses [handing out medication] was. That was the other thing, it took me a long fight to get my eye drops. I had to go to the hospital every four hours for my eye drops and asthma inhaler, and even though I didn't need them that often, I was still expected to go. The screw would shout 'Doses' and expect you to be waiting by the front door. For some obscure reason you had to be taken over. You went to work by yourself but you had to be taken to the hospital, and when I was on Martin it was right next door. So that was another thing to fit in. I never thought I'd be able to remember it all. It was very hectic.

Whilst I was in prison I only saw my daughter twice. I asked the probation department if they could arrange a visit as it didn't look like anyone else was going to. My probation officer outside told me she'd try to bring her up, but then she said it was too far and she couldn't get the funds, so I only saw her twice in eight months. On both occasions friends brought her. I asked the governor whether I could have a visit in the probation department so that Karen didn't have to see me in the gym with everyone else and I could talk to her a bit more intimately. I hadn't seen her since before the trial, I really wanted to reassure her and talk to her on her own, to help my relationship with her continue. I thought it would be much easier to see her in those sort of surroundings. But they weren't having any of it. It was mean, especially after all she'd been through.

What the visits were like depended on how full the gym was. We were allowed a visit every fortnight. On Wednesdays or Saturdays you got two hours (other days it was only thirty minutes) so obviously everyone came on those days. The fuller the gym was, the more isolated you were with your visitors, because you were in a crowd. You were allowed up to three visitors at a time and had to sit opposite them at individual tables. If the gym wasn't very full you were really conscious of the number of screws; they'd be all round the back, all round the perimeter, and there was apparently a spy hole over the basketball net which they watched through. They'd be going up and down between the aisles as well. There was a table at one end where a principal officer and a couple of others sat overseeing the whole lot. Wednesdays was the only day ex-inmates were allowed to visit friends in prison. If you saw someone you knew and you shouted out to them, you were in dead trouble, even if you shouted hello, or if you asked someone at the next table for a cigarette.

If anything had been brought in for you it had to be handed in at the screws' table, and they had to sign the property book. There were always great arguments about whether it was something you were allowed or not, and that always seemed to take up half the visit. Your poor visitors had come miles, had to wait to be taken from the prison gate to the gym, and then had to queue up waiting to hand in a bunch of flowers or something trivial, and then it all had to be signed for, then the screws came over to your table and *you* had to sign for it. On one occasion I had some winter clothes brought in and it did take up literally half the visit, sorting all that out, and arguing about what I could and couldn't have. Everything brought or sent in has first to go through 'property' and spend a few days (which usually become weeks) there before you eventually get it. All this ridiculous red tape! It's not surprising nobody has any respect for it. All these totally ludicrous things just make work for everyone, and the screws put pressure on the inmates with such pointless regulations as well as causing lots of paperwork for themselves.

I didn't get many visits. If you didn't have your fortnightly visit you were allowed a letter in lieu or sometimes a phone call. Only three people were allowed to make a phone call each week, which meant sometimes you had to wait your turn for weeks. Those phone calls could be very distressing, especially as there was always a screw hovering nearby listening to what you were saying and there was pressure to say everything in your allotted ten minutes. It just wasn't worth it, so I didn't bother to apply.

Prison is so petty. All the rules and regulations: I'm sure it's much worse for women than for men. Men wouldn't stand for it. One classic example was of a girl getting a pound fine and losing three days' remission for giving another girl a cigarette paper. (You are not allowed to give or lend anything at all: technically you're not even allowed to read each other's books!) She was only earning about £1.30 a week, so that was almost her entire wage. Lots of girls got put on report for wearing each other's clothes – usually for visits, when they'd want to borrow something that looked good. You were allowed so few clothes that it was nice to be able to wear something different. On houses where the screws were really strict about these things you had a locker check each week and if every single item wasn't in your locker you'd had it. Punishments generally seemed to get a lot more severe whilst I was there. People started losing weeks' rather than days' remission. Three girls lost two weeks for talking in the medicine queue whilst waiting for doses. Some screws would let you talk and some wouldn't, it was all very arbitrary. I remember when I'd been there only two weeks I almost got put on report for smoking in the avenue. I'd no idea you weren't allowed to until this huge screw bears down on me throwing a wobbler, going blue with rage.

A lot of the younger officers tended to be very career orientated, and far heavier and aggressive. Some were ex-police or ex-army or whatever. The older ones were more maternal, and far more reasonable on the whole, with exceptions. There was a really heavy little clique, the same ones that ousted the governor.* I felt the screws who didn't belong to this clique and didn't subscribe to it were given almost as hard a time by them as the inmates. The tough ones were certainly the dominant force within the prison. The older screws were dropping like flies. One particularly lovely lady called Mrs [S] who I used to talk to a lot had had enough, she was going. She couldn't stand it any more. Mrs [A] was another one. They were local women and had joined for a job, but they were grandmotherly in a way, just the sort of people the younger girls needed. Not these tough, heavy, very often butch young women who were incredibly disciplinarian and so uncaring and unbothered. They were incredibly sarcastic and mocking, and their general treatment of you was so demeaning. They'd delight in things like withholding the mail, or telling the cook off for making the food look too attractive or for giving people too much. Whatever they could stick their noses into they would, like telling you off if you had more than eight photos on your pin board. Why should it matter how many photos you had? Totally ridiculous things. They'd stir things up with lots of nasty sly remarks, especially to someone like me who wasn't doing anything tangible they could punish. I think they found women like me really hard to cope with. Being quite educated and articulate I wasn't the sort of prisoner they expected, even though as there are more drug offenders there are more and more women like me. There were about thirty

---

* The governor James Anderson was forced to leave Styal in March 1986. He came under heavy criticism from the officers who said he was too soft. Mr Anderson stated publicly that pregnant women should be paroled before confinement.

Black or non-English-speaking women, out of a population of about three hundred. They were mostly LTIs [long-term inmates] so I didn't see much of them. But those I did see seemed to have a harder time. There was only one Black officer.

There was one awful incident towards the end of my sentence. It had been a very hard and bitterly cold winter. The heating was woefully inadequate – upstairs there were just pipes running round the rooms, and downstairs a few scattered radiators. The houses had antiquated boiler systems, which constantly went wrong. They were in desperate need of repair, and there was never enough hot water to heat the pipes. Martin house was notoriously bad for often having no hot water. One day in February the boiler broke down; there'd been no heat or hot water all day. The women were told it would soon be mended, but by the time it came for bed it still wasn't repaired, although probably all it needed was a new fuse. There was always a couple of works men on call, so it could easily have been done. The screws had electric fires in their office, so it didn't bother them. At 9 p.m. the women sat down in the common room and said they weren't going to bed until the heating was fixed. A few minutes later they were given a direct order to go to bed – and if you disobey a direct order you're instantly put on report. It's quite a serious charge. Out of the twenty-eight women on the house, three went to bed, and they were in fact to lose two weeks' remission each for being in bed a few minutes late. The rest linked arms and said they were staying there until the heating was fixed. Various high-ranking people, ending up with the governor himself, turned up, asking them to go to bed, but they wouldn't go. After a while they were left alone for a bit and then a Black Maria turned up. A substantial number of police came out with truncheons, went into the house and very forcibly removed eight women and drove them off to Risley. One was seen being carried out, head down, legs back, bleeding copiously from the head. All the screws were there. One was handing out straps and the girls' hands and feet were strapped together before they were thrown in the van. There were police waiting for them in the van and they got another good beating.

All the screws were joining in, the girls were horribly out-numbered. They were just having a peaceful protest, sitting there and linking arms: no threats or fear of violence. The screws, it seemed, had picked out the eight most troublesome in the house, most of which were YCs. Out of them two eventually went to Durham. Only one came back to Styal, a few days after it all happened, and I bumped into her on my way to work. I said to her, 'Look I'm going out in a couple of weeks, you must tell me exactly what happened so I can tell the papers about it.' She was walking with a girl who was quite a problematic and attention-seeking sort of person. Anyway, she said she'd give me something about it on Sunday at NA [the Narcotics Anonymous Group which meets weekly at Styal]. The next day I was walking to work and I'd just got as far as the hospital. There's always screws standing outside there, like there's always screws lining the routes to work making sure you don't stop to talk to anyone. Anyway this woman, the problematic one, stopped me in full view of everyone and handed me this folded piece of paper. I stood and looked at her aghast, as there were at least half a dozen screws watching, and writing notes or letters to another prisoner is absolutely forbidden. I wasn't really thinking at the time. I was listening engrossed to the woman I was walking to work with, who the night before had found two night-screws stretched out on the desk in a passionate embrace when she'd gone downstairs to the office to ask for a Tampax. So I was miles away! I just looked at this piece of paper in horror and was pounced on. I never saw what it was, it was still folded. The screws were apoplectic with rage. 'What's the meaning of this?' 'I don't know.' I had no idea what it was. I was told to go off to work. I'd only been there about five minutes when they came to escort me off down to Bleak House, where I was stripped naked and given a blanket and put into a cell. Bleak House is sub-human. It's absolutely horrifying – makes Holloway look like a holiday camp. The cells are completely bare, some with an iron bedframe bolted to the floor, others with only a mattress and plastic bowl, pot, and that's it. It was freezing cold. I was eventually given my clothes back, but they were all muddy and damp because I'd been on gardens. I didn't get my proper clothes, or any sheets, for over twenty-four hours.

The screws who worked down on the block were absolute monsters. I suppose it takes a pretty special sort of screw to be able to work in those conditions, to choose to work down there, but they were totally inhuman. And it was like being new to prison all over again, the rules and regulations were quite different. You were let out four times a day for slop-out, when they came round with the trolley and collected the plates. There was no toilet paper in the cell, so you had to ask for it. You're allowed very little of your own stuff down there, just a set of clothes, but it all goes down just in case you don't return to your house. All the contents of my locker had been tipped into a blanket. Some women were kept down there for weeks, some in the special cells, with strip dress, paper plates, paper pot. It could drive you mad. I'm sure it's not allowed to keep people in solitary for long periods. I'm sure they are breaking the rules.

I was hauled off in front of the assistant governor for adjudication. He sits behind a desk and you stand a few feet away with a screw facing you really close on either side. 'You realise what this is?' I hadn't realised what it was at all, presumably a note. I said, 'It was put in my hand. I don't know. Do you think I'd be stupid enough to do something like that in full view of everyone? I'm going home in a couple of weeks.' 'Oh no you're not, we're going to get your parole revoked. This is a very serious case.' If I'd less sense than I have, I'd have believed them. I'd have been suicidal. I knew it was just idle threats, but a lot wouldn't have – they'd have been distraught. I think I was set up. The screws knew I was vocal and articulate and had by then got my own way to a fair extent by being incredibly polite and incredibly persistent but not actually stepping out of line. I'm sure I was set up and this girl was exactly the sort of person they'd be able to get to do it, because there was no sense in it otherwise. Maybe the note said something about my going to the newspapers. I don't know, as I never saw it. But there was no sense in her giving it to me in full view of everyone. To cut a long story short, I was given an additional three days behind the door, with a £1 fine for being in receipt of an illegal letter, even though it was put into my hand. I didn't know what it was and I certainly hadn't asked for it.

Prison teaches you a lot of new tricks. It teaches you a severe disregard for the entire system. I saw people who came in pretty straight but who changed their attitudes and opinions drastically. It did nothing but harm and didn't help anyone. There doesn't seem to be any emphasis on rehabilitation or help in any respect. It was okay painting window frames, but it wasn't going to help me get a job when I got outside.

My daughter still lives with her father. She had settled there to some extent by the time I was released and I didn't think it was good to disrupt her again. I decided to put all these experiences to positive use and managed to get a job with a charitable trust in London which works with women ex-prisoners. I go back to Chelmsford most weekends and manage to see my daughter quite regularly, though our relationship is still nothing like as close as it was before my arrest. I have to remember we spent her first ten years together and hope that this will be what matters in the long run. To be honest, though, this separation has broken my heart. I don't think it's something I'll ever really get over.

Margy

Margy was twenty-seven when we spoke with her and was living in a one-bedroomed flat in Newcastle-upon-Tyne with her three-year-old daughter Donna, her second child. Although she felt she had settled down a lot since her last release from prison, she was still having difficulties coping with the day-to-day strain and isolation of being a single parent. She had been out of prison for four years but was on two suspended sentences for shoplifting, and had recently been arrested for shoplifting again. It looked almost certain she would face another prison sentence in the near future.

Margy comes from Newcastle and speaks with a Geordie accent. We didn't want to change her words, but should perhaps explain that Geordies often use 'us' instead of 'me'.

I can remember being taken into care when I was three. I can remember being in the back of a car and I was screaming. The social worker was driving. Me dad had hit us with a belt, that's why I ended up in a home.

I can't remember seeing me dad till I was five. They'd sent us home to see if I could live with me mam and dad, but it didn't last long. Me dad still used to batter us, so me and me brothers and sisters all got put back into care. They put us all in different homes and I can't remember the whole family being together, ever. It used to make me really mad because some of me brothers and sisters used to get put in the same homes together, but I was always on my own.

They used to move us round from one home to another all the time. I don't know why. I was in one home for three years when I was at junior school. It was a family group home and we used to call the staff 'mam' and 'dad'. I was dead happy there and then, all of a sudden, they came one day and just moved me to another home. They never told me why and that really hurt. That's when I started running away and getting into trouble.

They never put us in foster care. I don't know why. When I was running away they put me in an approved school for girls run by nuns. I was there three years. They were dead strict. I ran away loads of times but they kept taking us back. I hated it. You were supposed to get home leaves but every time I was due for mine they used to stop it. I felt as though they were picking on me, trying to cause trouble so they'd have a reason for stopping me home leave. One Christmas I hit one of the nuns and they expelled me. I went home to me mam, who had left me dad by then. That was when I was fifteen. Me and me mam didn't get on, we started fighting and then I started shoplifting. That was how I got remanded in custody when I was only fifteen. I reckon most of the kids I knew in care ended up in trouble.

When I was put in the police cells after getting remanded, the police were trying to scare us, telling us about lesbians and all that at Low Newton remand centre. They said that if I was cheeky at Low Newton the screws would just hit me. When I got there I thought it was all right. It wasn't really that different from the approved school. In a place like that it all depends how you get on with the screws: some lasses did take hell. When I went to court I pleaded guilty, and I didn't get a sentence, so I was out again. I was still under a care order so the Social Services put me in a hostel. I only stayed a couple of days and then I ran away to London. I thought it would be great down there, but I started having a bad time so I went back to Newcastle. I had nowhere to go and I kept getting thrown out of places. They even hoyed [threw] us out of the Salvation Army hostel. It wasn't long before I got caught shoplifting again so I was back on remand at Low Newton – I think I must have been on remand there about eight times. I walked out of court after that one too.

I got my first borstal when I was about eighteen for assault on another girl. There were some young lasses in the Chilli [Chillingham Arms], they were talking about my tattoos and that and staring at me, so I had a fight with one of them. I got six months to two years borstal, and I was at Bullwood Hall for about nine months. Bullwood Hall is in Essex so I was three hundred miles away from Newcastle. When I first went in, I was on like an assessment unit. I was there a few days and then me and me friends barricaded ourselves in a cell and we wouldn't come out because there was nowt to do. The screws kept coming to try and get us out, sweet-talking us all nice and that, but we wouldn't come out. Then they got the bloke screws in. The blokes tried to get us out with water – the firehoses. They put water through the window and then got the door down, just knocked it down. Then they put us in the block. It was horrible. We were just locked up all the time, with half an hour exercise a day and no books to read. We just had to sit there all day on our own, and I was in for a couple of weeks.

Then I was put back onto the house. I can't remember very much about that. They were nearly all young ones where I was. The older ones used to like bully the young ones if you were soft and that, and like take your tabs [cigarettes] and threaten you, things like that. I was in with them, you know, the bullies. At first I was scared, but after a while I got used to it. One lass, she tried to hang herself because of the bullying. She got picked on 'cause she was soft and she was daft. They used to pinch her tabs and everything, so she tried to hang herself.

During the day there was a factory and you used to have to make boxes, or if you were a cleaner you used to have to scrub the landings and everything, or there was a farm and you could work there – but you used to have to be really trusted to work on that. I was in the factory making boxes and it was dead boring. I made a lot of friends at Bullwood Hall. After I came out I was going to write to them, but I never bothered. One of them wrote to me, but I never wrote back. Some of the screws were all right, but it all depends on how you got on with them. I was on report another time too. I refused to go in my cell and they put us down the block. They put us in the padded room overnight. Then another time I smashed my cell up and slashed my arms and that, because I didn't get any letters or anything like that, so one of the screws came in and they put us down the block. I was there for two weeks. No one really bothered that I didn't get any letters or visits. I didn't expect my family to visit me because it was too far, but they could have wrote.

There was quite a lot on drugs – a lot on tranquillisers. On the hospital they were all doped up. If you got a headache or anything, the nurse would just give you daft little tablets for it. When I was at Bullwood Hall I was on Triptazol [a tranquilliser] for me temper. When they give you it, they have to watch you swallow it, but I used to keep it in the back of my throat and save it up. Then I took the tablets all at once. I wasn't trying to kill myself. I don't know why I did it. I was just trying to get a buzz. I was bad for about a week. I was padded up with me mate and she says I just went weird. She was dead frightened and was pressing on the bell and everything, but nobody came that night. I was bad for ages. It happens a lot that you ring the bell and they just don't come. They never found out I'd done it.

I got out of Bullwood Hall on a Tuesday and I was picked up on the Thursday, two days later, for robbery. It was robbery with violence. I robbed a bloke in the park with two of me mates, a lad and a lass. They got picked up as well. We were kept in the police station for a couple of days and then we got remanded to Low Newton. While I was there they found out I'd fallen pregnant while I was on my home leave from Bullwood Hall. We were on remand for about three months and then we were up at the Crown court. I got a fresh whack of borstal, the lad got borstal and the other lass got fifteen months' prison. When I got sent down the judge said, 'You should be out for the baby's birth', but I wasn't.

After I was at court I had to go back to Low Newton to wait for a few weeks before I could go to Styal prison. If I hadn't been pregnant I would have been sent back to Bullwood, but they haven't got a mother and baby unit there, though in those days Styal was only for women over twenty-one, apart from the pregnant borstal girls.

I was terrified because I had never been in a proper prison before, and I had heard about Styal. I had heard that the lasses used to beat you up when you first got in and that the lesbians used to grab hold of you and that there was loads of violence and everything. I was really scared. It was true for some people, because if you act soft when you go in, they do pick on you, but when I got there I knew how to act from being in Bullwood Hall and other places. I was on the assessment house to start with, waiting to go on another house.

The lesbians didn't bother me. You can easily get done for lesbian activities. People used to lose a lot of time for that. If you've got a mate, a best mate, and she's on a different house, you'll write her a note because you hardly ever see her, and if you get caught for that you lose a couple of weeks. I got done for that. I don't know why they are so strict, because a lot of the screws are lesbians. If they knew you were friendly with someone, they would try their hardest to separate you. They would put you on different jobs so you'd hardly see one another.

I had to go to Fox House, the pregnant house. I didn't like that. There were far too many of us and I kept getting depression and that, with being pregnant. We went to the outside hospital for the ante-natal clinic. They took us a few at a time and there were always prison officers with us. We had to sit in the waiting room with everyone else. Everyone knew we were from the prison, they stared at us. The doctors and nurses knew too and just treated you any old way. We had to go to classes as well. It was just like being back at school. We had sewing classes and cookery. They never taught you nowt. You knew with being pregnant, if you were sick or anything, you still had to go to classes. One time I refused to go 'cause I was bad. It was before I had the bairn, and I wouldn't go and they put us down the block for being cheeky.

I was down there two days. When I came up they put us in the detention room on the house for pregnant women. It was my first night back and I was getting pains and everything. There's a nurse who sleeps in the house, and one of the lasses knocked for her to come and look at us. She came and examined us and she says, 'Oh, you're all right.' I was screaming, I was saying, 'I'm in labour', and she says, 'You'll be okay – if it gets any worse give us another knock.' I knocked again and she was going off it, going really crazy at me. She thought I was carrying on, and she didn't think I was in labour. In the end they got an ambulance and rushed us to hospital and they said it was a good job they did. I had the bairn straight away. If I had gone into labour a couple of days earlier, I would have been on my own, down the block, with no nurse, nobody. They knew I was ready to drop the bairn.

When I had the baby, Stephen, the screws left me in the outside hospital but they took my clothes. They take everything away. I was in a big ward all on my own. Everyone knew I was from prison. When I had the bairn, they wanted us back to the prison the day after, but I was haemorrhaging and the doctor says, 'There's no way she can go back now.' So they kept us in a few days.

When I got back I had bed rest for a couple of days and then they had me scrubbing the houses and that. They made us scrub all the way through pregnancy as well, right up to the end. They used to say it was good for you. The doctor was really bad. He didn't care. I had post-natal depression, and I was tired and everything. I was breastfeeding and the bloke screws used to walk in the room. There was a big, fat screw there, and he was always walking in and out. The way they treated me in the mother and baby unit, it didn't seem as though it was my baby. They used to tell me what to do with it. I could only see him when they said I could, and they would be stood right next to me, watching me all the time. I had to do what they told me to do. We had to put the babies down at a certain time and leave them – it was horrible.

The bairn started bringing his milk back up all the time when he was just a few days old. This was going on for a couple of days, so I was getting worried and I took him to the prison doctor and he says, 'It might be with you breastfeeding, try him on the bottle.' So I tried the bottle and he was still vomiting all the time. By this time I was really getting worried, so I took him back and the doctor said, 'Oh, it's all right, there's nothing the matter with him.' I said I wanted him to go to an outside hospital, so they took him. I was eating my tea that afternoon – they wouldn't let me go too – and I got called over to the Centre [the prison officers' operational centre within the prison]. That's where they give you good news or bad news. The priest was there and everything, and he told us to sit down. He says, 'Stephen's got to have an emergency operation, so you've got to go to the hospital to sign the forms.' They had no sympathy or nowt. So I just cracked up.

They didn't tell us what the operation was for. They took us to the hospital and I had to sign the paper and that was it. They let us see him for a couple of minutes, and then they took us back to the prison. He had the operation the next day and they took us for a couple of minutes and that was it – they just didn't care. I lost a lot of time [lost remission as a punishment for breaking the rules], what with the bairn and everything. I just cracked up, and they put us down the block. I was smashing everything up and setting about people, 'cause I didn't know what was going on or nothing. They gave us some time back afterwards, because of the bairn having an operation. [Lost remission can be restored later, following a period of good behaviour.] I think the only reason they gave us time back was because I was going to report the prison doctor to the Board of Visitors.

When Stephen was in hospital they kept us on the same house with all the mothers and babies, even though I had asked to be off it. That really did upset us. He was in hospital for nearly a month, and I never saw him until the day I got out. No one talked to us about him. The only person who ever explained what the operation was for was the nurse at the hospital, or I would never have known. It wasn't a very dangerous operation, but they never told me that.

On the day I got out they picked us up in a taxi at the prison and then we went to the hospital to pick him up. Then they put us in the Fleming Hospital in Newcastle, me and the bairn, because I had nowhere else to go. I didn't like it there, so my mother came to see me and when she seen the bairn she just says, 'Come home.' So I went home with her. After a couple of days, me and me mother weren't getting on, so she hoyed me out. She was after keeping the bairn. I took him, though, and I went to live with some friends. Our Mickey [Margy's brother] came looking for us and he kicked me and took the bairn away. He said it would just be until I got myself sorted out, and then I would get him back straight away. The next thing I knew Stephen was with foster parents. Mickey had rang up the social worker and he had taken the bairn. A couple of days later I was that fed up I got myself in trouble. I started shoplifting again and then I was on remand. I was at Low Newton a couple of weeks and then I got out on bail and went to see Stephen, but then I got lifted again, back to Low Newton.

While I was on bail and Stephen was still with foster parents, they promised I could have Stephen for Christmas. I had bought him loads of toys. I was living at my friend's down at Forest Hall [in Newcastle]. She had done all the house out and got all the presents and everything, but then they says I couldn't have him or see him. The same social worker wanted Donna taken off us at birth. They never gave us a chance with Stephen. They knew what I was like with me mother. They knew we didn't get on, and they never tried to get us a flat or nowt, so when I got out of prison with him I was just on my own. I reckon if I had had a flat and everything I could have given it a try. Stephen might have made me settle down like Donna has.

I got a sentence and was sent back to Styal. I only saw Stephen a few times before I went back to prison. It used to upset me. The social worker I had at the time kept coming to see me in Low Newton and saying, 'Do you not think it's best if you get him adopted?' When I got sent down, all through my sentence, the social worker kept coming to see us. When I got out of prison again I went to a hostel in Manchester and he was coming up there all the time. I was getting that sick I ended up signing the papers and Stephen was adopted. I signed the papers in

Manchester and after that I never seen the social worker again. He was saying he would come up and tell us how Stephen was and everything. The social worker never talked about me getting Stephen back. I don't think he wanted me to have him back, with us being in prison and that. He used to write to me about how it was best for Stephen if he got adopted, 'cause I didn't know what I was going to do with me life, I wasn't settled and I'd probably end up back in prison. I think I was pressured into signing the papers. As soon as I signed them, I never heard from him anymore. He promised us photos of the bairn because I said that was the condition for signing, and I got one and that was that. I heard nowt more. I was never given the chance to write Stephen a letter explaining why I gave him up for when he is older or anything.

During that last sentence I was at Styal again and then at Askham Grange. I had been in Styal for a few months and I kept putting in for an open prison, but they kept saying no. In the end, they shipped us out because I was going to complain about the doctor. I was working on the gardens and we had to sweep all the grounds. I had conjunctivitis and I was trying to get off work because my eyes were really bad. I shouldn't have been where there was dust and that. The doctor sent us back to work even though my eyes were really bad. The Board of Visitors were coming round and I was going to tell them, so that's why they shipped us out to Askham Grange open prison. That's twice they done that sort of thing. I'd done nearly all me time in Styal, you know, and then the last thing they sent us out.

Askham Grange wasn't like a prison. The first day me and me friend got inside the doors we didn't know where to go. Nobody told us. You hardly ever seen the screws or nowt. The first day we just hated it, but when we got used to it, it was nowt like a prison. In some ways it was better and in some ways it was worse. If you wanted to, you could have just went, the doors were just open. There was a lot of temptation. There was no screws to stop violence and fighting and all that, you could have just killed somebody. There was a lot of fights and bullying of the soft lasses. In other ways it was really petty and you could get nicked for daft little things. I wasn't at Askham Grange for very long, just to finish off my sentence.

There are lots of really bad things about prison. It's really degrading – they go out of their way to upset you. In Styal we used to get searched, sometimes strip searched. Strip searching made me feel terrible – I was dead embarrassed. You just have to stand there. Then you have to go and have a bath and see the nurse, and she checks your hair and they check you for VD. At Bullwood Hall the doctor checks you for VD after home leaves, too. It's an internal examination, and you've got to have it. If you don't, you're locked in until you will. You just have to have it.

It's bad when you get your period in prison. You've got to tell them when you're on and ask for sanitary towels. It's dead embarrassing. They give you one at a time. If you ask for Tampax they have to write down how many, because you can use the wrapping paper for roll-ups. If you are on heavy and you need more, they just say, 'What do you need all those for?' It was really embarrassing. If you needed a new sanitary towel in the night you couldn't get one. You couldn't ring the bell or they would go mad.

We used to have a bath once a week. That's another thing. If you're on really heavy, you need a bath or you'll smell and that, but you couldn't – one a week. When we did get a bath it was really quick – just in and out. In Low Newton, in the new part, there was wash-basins in the cell, but it's still embarrassing if you're sharing a cell and you want a strip wash. Slopping-out is disgusting. I used to have bad pains because I wouldn't go on the bucket at night. You were only allowed to wash your clothes once a week. You had to wash your underwear in your cell at night. In the old cells you had to take a bucket of water in, get a wash, and then wash your underwear in it, in the same bucket. The sheets got changed once a week, but you could change more often if you got blood on them or something. But some of the lasses were too embarrassed to say. You had to book to get your hair cut, your toenails cut and your fingernails cut, and a screw had to stand and watch you with the scissors. You had to go on

Governor's app [put in an application to the Governor] to ask to get your toenails cut. The food was disgusting as well. I just couldn't eat it. If you didn't like it, that was it. You would just starve. I never felt I had enough food when I was pregnant.

One of the worst places is Bleak House at Styal, the punishment block. It's scruffy and rotten. One lass went down and she had some glass or something, and she was threatening to slash her wrists and there was a screw shouting, 'Well do it.' She did like, she cut herself. They don't care. A lass in Low Newton hanged herself the second time I was in there. I was only two cells away from her. She was just in for a fine and it was her first time. I did most of my tattoos in prison. I did a few while I was out, but most of them in prison. I got nicked for it at Low Newton. A lot of the girls put tattoos on. I did it out of boredom, it was something to do, and for status. If you were good friends with another lass, you would get each other's names put on.

I was in Styal prison over Christmas once and it was dead depressing. They gave us a lollipop, off the screws, one each. I think they were just taking the piss. It's worse for the lasses with kids at Christmas. There's more fights then, everyone loses their tempers. There were a lot of fights anyway, most of them were over jealousy about friendships, also over tobacco. Some of the lasses would kill for tab-ends and that. The screws half the time would leave tab-ends on purpose and there were fights over who would have them. It's degrading. We rolled up tea leaves, leaves, everything.

It's really boring being in prison as well. I didn't read much, but I tried to read the Bible in Bullwood Hall. There was one in the cell. I didn't get very far with it. You are only allowed ten photographs and if you want any more you have to put some in your property [stored property inaccessible to the prisoner] or hand them out. That was really bad for people with kids. It was worse all round for people with kids: they can't back-answer anybody. They can't afford to lose time because they've got to be out for the bairns. But if you don't do what the other lasses tell you to, you're called a softie or a shit or something like that. You just cannot win.

I don't really keep in touch with anyone from prison now. I used to write a bit, but not now. I feel embarrassed about people knowing I was in prison. A couple of years ago I wasn't bothered who knew. It's embarrassing when you get out, too. In Newcastle most of the people know us and all the lads would say, 'Oh, you lesbian' and all that. My brothers all said that. I'm the only girl in the family that's been in prison. They never used to come and see us much. They come once to Styal, they didn't come to Bullwood Hall, and I think they came to Askham Grange once. I think it would have been better to get community work instead of prison – something to do. That was the problem – boredom. So I used to drink and get into trouble.

I've been in prison for assault, robbery, shoplifting and burglary. When I was in prison I wasn't hard to start with, but I soon got that way. I used to pick on some of the soft ones to survive. I just try to forget it all now, but I might have to go back. I would hate that 'cause I would lose Donna. The women in prison who had kids were always dead upset. People who were going in for fines and just daft shoplifting and that were getting their bairns taken away. It's not only them that suffer – it's the bairns as well. Prison just made me worse; it did nowt else. I mean you learn things off the others. I wasn't frightened of it. Sometimes, in a sort of way, I was glad to be in, when I couldn't cope on the outside. I was used to it. I didn't have to make any decisions. It's when you get out that the problems really start. It's just since I had Donna that things have been different for me.

When Margy eventually went to court for her new shoplifting charge the judge gave her a probation order. She freely admitted that when she was shoplifting she was, in a way, hoping to go to prison. Because of the enormous disruptions she had suffered in her life she was finding it difficult to manage on a day-to-day basis, and prison represented a way of 'escaping' from her immediate problems. But as soon as she was arrested the potential consequences really came home to her. Donna was taken into foster care at the end of 1986, and there seems little prospect of her returning to live with Margy in the near future.

Adaku

Adaku was living alone on the seventeenth floor of a tower block in South London when we spoke to her.

I was born in this country in 1964. In 1974 I went back to Nigeria with my parents. I lived with my father, then when my father died I came back to this country. I had an argument with my mother and I just ran away from home and came here without telling her. I knew one person in London. I thought she was a friend but when I got here she had changed. She said I couldn't stay with her, that her aunty was in the house, things like that, so I had nowhere to go. The night I arrived I was walking around the streets on my own looking for work. I found work but I didn't tell them I had nowhere to stay, that when it was night time, I got on the night buses and stayed there until morning and then went back to work. Sometimes I was sacked because I was late, sometimes because I was so tired. I worked in kitchen jobs, Pizza Huts. I never stayed in one job for longer than a month.

I started riding on the buses in August and did it until November. I got on the buses at Trafalgar Square, it took me to the other end and brought me back again, and I got down and got on another one. I didn't know where I was going. No one stopped me to ask me what I was doing. I was afraid at first, but then I got used to it. But the cold was too much. Then I lost all my things, someone stole them. I went to a hostel in

Hampstead. They said I could only stay one week, but I stayed there for two, and they didn't know. Then I had a boyfriend and I went to stay with him. I'd met him in Nigeria. His father was staying in the same house, and didn't know I was staying there, so I used to creep in at night. I was sleeping with my boyfriend, and after a few months I found I was pregnant and I had to stop going there. So I went to the council, I didn't know anything about social security, even that there was such a thing, so I was given benefit and a hostel to stay in at Elephant and Castle.

I have a Nigerian passport and a British passport. But because I didn't tell my mother I was coming here, I couldn't get my British passport. When they asked me why I didn't have a British passport that's when the immigration problems started. They asked me to report to them every week, but I didn't go, and they stopped my benefit.

I started getting into trouble. I went to Marks and Spencer and stole some clothes, and then I stole some other things – I was short of money. For the first offence I was given a fine. On the second offence I was given a suspended sentence. The third offence, that was after the immigration problems, I was sent to prison. I was on remand for three weeks. My fourth offence I spent another three weeks on remand, and my fifth offence I spent one month. They were all for stealing from shops. I was sent to Holloway prison.

The first time I went to prison I had already had the baby, but he was taken away from me in hospital. I'd told them I had immigration problems and that they'd stopped my benefit. My social worker who gave me advice asked if I wanted adoption or fostering, and I said fostering (it was a white family). Then I went to prison and they made the baby a ward of court without telling me. My solicitor got some papers for me to sign, but I was so depressed I didn't know what it was about. When I came out, they told me the court dates of when he was going to be adopted. It was against my will but I felt there was no use fighting it, because the social worker had many things against me, like my not going to see the baby, and my being in prison – there were many things against me.

When I first went to Holloway, I was frightened by the look of the screws: some are fat and tall. Some look at you as if, well, you're not important. When you go in, they search you and look at your files, in front of you. If you're in for drugs, they pull your clothes off, tell you to turn round and do all sorts of things to you. I wasn't in for drugs, so I didn't get that treatment. I was told to sit down for about five hours in a hall, to wait for them to call my name out, to go to see the doctor. He doesn't even ask what's wrong with you, he doesn't want to know. He just tries to shut you down. If you tell him you have a pain in your chest, he just says, 'Well it's because you came to prison, that's why you have the pain.' He doesn't give you medication, nothing at all. Every time I get caught or arrested I get asthma. I took my inhaler with me, and they took it off me, telling me I used it to make myself high. I was afraid I'd have an attack. There were other girls there who were on drugs, who were unhappy or sick, but still they didn't do anything.

Even if you're dying in prison, the screws don't want to know. If you press the bell because of a headache, they say, 'Don't ring the bell unless you're dying.' Things like that. If there's a fight, they tie your hands, pull your head sideways and put you down the block. A person can spend about five days there, just in the dark. I went down there once when I had a fight with a girl, a white girl. She called me a Black bitch. Something happened and she just said it, then she hit me and I had to hit her back. They took both of us down the block, and we were there for two days – no blankets, no bed, nothing, just a mattress on the floor. They took all my own clothes and gave me a nightgown. You're not allowed tobacco in there either. You're not allowed anything to make you happy, not even books. You're given what they want to give you.

On the morning of the third day we went to the prison court where the governor sits. That was the governor of Holloway – a man. Two screws stand right in front of you. Sometimes he will punish you. You might be locked up for a long time, or you might be given a fine, which is taken out of your weekly allowance. Sometimes they might just give you a caution. I got a caution, and told not to do it again. After that, you're taken back upstairs, but to a different wing and a different room. You're not taken to the same wing because they think you might fight again.

Some of the other women were good, some of them bad. They didn't like newcomers, and didn't behave well towards them. I was afraid when I first went because I thought that people who go to prison, they're bad. But some of them are nice.

After three weeks, I went to court and was put on probation. About two or three months after that, I got into trouble again and was taken back to prison. I was on remand all the time. I've never been sentenced. When you plead guilty and you get sent in on remand, then you get treated like a sentenced prisoner, because you're guilty. But when the judge doesn't ask you to plead, and you're not guilty, you're treated like a person who's sent to prison for a crime that she hasn't committed.

I knew when I got into trouble I might get sent back, because when you've been to prison once, you can be sent back every time you get into trouble. The police don't let you go, once you've been to prison. I was sent to prison for five weeks. That was the time I started to get used to the place, to the screws and things like that, because some had seen me before.

Some of the screws try to annoy you. Once you've done something wrong, they try to get you to do something wrong again and lose your remission. That's what they want. I didn't want that to happen. I didn't want to get into trouble.

Some of the screws are normal people, though. I was talking to a screw one day and she was telling me that when she'd wanted to get work in prison she thought she'd be there to help prisoners. But when she got to prison all her mates were telling her, 'No, no, you don't talk to a prisoner like that, you talk to her sharp.' They told her you don't respect the prisoners, you must always be strict, so any time she wanted to talk to a girl and one of her mates was there she had to pretend. But when nobody was there she changed to her normal self again.

I am a Christian. I like the church in prison. But the prisoners themselves don't use the church as it should be used. They crack jokes, laughing and shouting. The screws don't use it properly either. They're not supposed to beat people or judge people in church. They should let us get out of church and then get the people they want instead of grabbing the person they want right in the middle of the church and carrying them out.

I don't like anything to do with drugs. If I see a person is charged and sentenced because of drugs, I don't really like them because I think that's why there is more crime in this country. People who say they sell drugs because they don't have enough money, I think they're lying. I think they want fast money. If you do a crime and get about thirty pounds, that's about enough for one week. But they want thousands of pounds in a week. What's bad about this is that they don't take drugs – they've never touched them – but they want to sell them. I've asked many people I've met who sell drugs if they take them and they say, 'No, no'. So I say, 'Why do you bring drugs for other people to take?' It's bad.

In prison you have to get up by seven o'clock, and make your bed before breakfast. You have to clean your rooms out, scrub, polish. If you don't do that, you get put on report. After breakfast, we go back to our rooms and get locked up until it's time for dinner. Sometimes, if the screws are happy, they let us out for a while, and sometimes we have exercise after dinner. But most of the time you don't have exercise. Then you get locked up again – that might be till the end of the day.

I got books from the library to read. Sometimes I got a radio put on. If you're with five other women, at least two will complain. But if it's a room with one girl, it's okay. I didn't have education. They told me that the people they want for education are the people who are sentenced for about six months, not the ones who are only there for one month. If you're lucky you can work – like clean the floors of the passage, cook, wash pillowcases and clothes. There isn't work for everybody, so people who work are mostly the lucky ones. They don't get locked up. I worked in the kitchen scrubbing the pans. We used to get about £3 a week. The people who don't work get £1 a week. You buy cigarettes with that – they sell anything in ones. They sell sugar, twenty-five pence or ten pence.

People who are on remand are allowed a visit every day, for fifteen minutes. You can ask for the visits to be extended, but before you get that you're taken to the governor and asked why you want it longer and who is coming to visit you. If it's your boyfriend, it's 'Why do you want to spend more than fifteen minutes with your boyfriend?' But say it's your mother, or your probation officer or someone like that, it's all right. I wasn't afraid of losing my boyfriend while I was in prison, because I've seen people who've been in for two years and their boyfriends still come and see them. So why should it happen to me? I wasn't afraid of that. But we don't have any privacy. They read your letters, and if you write in your own language they bring back your letter and ask you to write it in English. If you can't write in English it's just too bad. If you have a letter come in with information that's wrong, they don't give it to you. They tell you you've got a letter but they've sent it back. And if you write a letter they don't like, they bring it back and want to know why you've written certain things. They don't want you to say anything about prison. You can't write names, or mention people you've met in prison – you can write about your friends, but not any names. And if someone writes in another language, you won't get it for a long time. They don't trust anybody in prison.

I think I was treated differently because I'm Black. Like, if you ask for a bath, they'll say, 'No, you can't have a bath.' You ask why, and they say, 'Don't ask me why, I said you can't have a bath.' A white woman asks for a bath, and they go and give her the key to the bathroom, things like that. If a Black woman is on a visit, they tend to search her more, watch her more, because they believe Blacks are too bad. It's difficult for Black people to get the things they need in prison. Some Black women use bleaching creams. Sometimes you can get it, but they make it too expensive so you can't afford to buy it. I have to have something to put on my legs – I have very dry skin – but I couldn't get that either. When I came out I was an awful colour.

White people are given things straight when they come in – shampoo, comb, brush. The shampoo and combs are for white people's hair; they don't have Black combs. I think there were about three Black officers. Most of the nurses are Black, though. The young ones were all right but the older ones were horrible.

Some of the Black girls are pretty powerful. There are a lot of Black people in prison. It's because of racism. Store detectives will watch a Black person more than a white person. I've been to Oxford Circus, stayed there from one o'clock to four o'clock, wandering about. A policeman comes and says, 'I've seen you wandering about from one o'clock to four o'clock, can we search your handbag, please?' What does he think I'm doing, selling drugs? I said, 'No.' I said he had no right. He said could I come to the station. I said 'No.' Then he called a policewoman, and a policewoman came, and I went to the station, and they searched me, and let me go. No apology, nothing. It's frightening. Even if a Black girl has nothing on her, it frightens her to death.

It's difficult for a Black girl to get a credit card. If you want to get money out it's harder than it is for white people – they always check you and go away and phone. I tried to apply for a credit card, but they refused me. And I tried to open a Giro bank account, and I put Mrs — [Nigerian surname]. When the letter came back, they put: 'We are sorry, we can't do it.' They don't tell you why they refuse you, but I think it was because they knew I was Black from my name. You have to be rich to get a card when you're Black. My father, before he died, he had an account in this country. He had about £1,000 in it. I went and said, 'I'm the daughter of Mr —. Before he died he gave me his statements to look after.' I showed them my birth certificate, but they still didn't believe me. I didn't go back. I couldn't do anything about it. I think many Black people turn bitter because of all this.

I've always wished that I never came back to this country. When my father died there were a lot of quarrels between my mother and I. I'd always lived with my father, so I didn't know her, or how she wanted me to be. There was a lot of quarrels about me going out, and not coming back till late. She locked me out, things like that, said I shouldn't go out, I should do this and that, all that kind of rubbish. I've got five sisters; she wasn't the same with them. Then I thought it was important not being allowed to go out and things. How I wished I'd stayed there! I should have been back at school in Nigeria. I passed my A levels, I did well. If I was back there I would have done something. I can't go back now because in Africa you can't go back without any qualifications. That's why I've applied for school in September. I want to go to school and get qualifications.

People look down on you, once you've been to prison. You can't do the course you want to do. They say, 'Have you been in trouble before?' 'Yes, I've been in trouble.' And you get a letter two days later: 'I'm sorry, we can't take you because you've been to prison.' This is why people who have committed crimes don't want to study: they can't do this, they can't do that. But I want to study.

I couldn't adapt to conditions in this country. I think that's what got me into crime. I never thought about going into shops and stealing other people's things before I came here; that never crossed my mind. But when I came to this country . . . Like here you go in the bank, and sign. You get the statement, the balance. It's not yours, but because you've got the signature right, you might withdraw everything. In Africa you can't do that. There when you go to the bank, you have to sit down for about two hours before they even think you're there. And if there's any slight mistake in the signature, they tell you, 'No, we can't give you this.' I think that's why people here do more crime. Things are made too easy for them. I've got friends who have done banks, but I don't do them. What I might do is steal credit cards and use them. That's what I got prison for the last time. A credit card came through my door. Not mine. I opened it and found it wasn't signed, so I signed it and used it. The way to crime here is easy. In Africa life is hard, but you can't go to crime. You can't go into a shop and steal. The shops are so small that the person in the shop sees every corner, though there are no cameras. I think if I went back to Africa I wouldn't even think of stealing.

I also think prison makes you better at crime. When I was in prison I learnt many things about cheques and cards. People talk about it and you learn, and you might do it when you get out. When I came out, one time, they didn't give me any money because I was on remand. So I was without money for about three weeks. The DHSS reckoned someone was signing on for me while I was in prison. I don't know who it was. They thought I sent them. So they didn't pay me.

The last time when I went to court I got an order to go to the day training centre at Camberwell for offenders who keep on getting into trouble. So I go there every day now, except Wednesday, my day off. That's for twelve weeks. I've done three weeks. Nine more weeks left. It's quite nice. People talk about their problems, and the probation officers are very good. Meals are good. I'm very worried, though, about when the twelve weeks is up, because I want to change, you see. I can see that I am changing, right, but I don't know what will happen when it's finished. That's worrying. In the day centre, they help you to get into college, or to get work, things like that. The Wednesdays off, they expect you to go and find work. They're training us now, to get up in the morning, to go to the centre. If you're late, the first time it's a director's warning, then two other warnings. After that, you go back to court. So people have to be there every day. If you're sick you have to get a medical certificate. I think it is like a prison, but it's better. People tell you to do this, but they're very friendly. I just hope I can get into college.

I am very worried now because I was on a deportation order, the immigration hadn't been settled. But when the immigration people came I got a letter, and they said that I could stay while they finished their inquiries. I'm not really worried about that, seeing as I was born in this country, but what I don't understand is why they should doubt me. If I wanted to sue the immigration people I would. I would make them pay for what they've done. They're still giving me hassles that I'm not British and they're going to deport me. They're just being difficult. What they told me was that people come to this country impersonating other people, get a passport and then pretend they're British.

I don't feel awkward with friends, because I only tell people who I think will understand. My boyfriend understands. He meets people who've been to prison, but not all of them are criminals. Two days after I met him I went to prison. Some people do tend to run away from you, they're afraid of you because they think you're wild. But not everybody is wild. To tell you the truth, before I went to prison I used to meet people who had been to prison and I didn't want to talk to them because I thought they were funny. But now I think, just because I've been to prison there's nothing wrong with me. I don't think I'm a criminal.

I think it's worse for a woman than a man. I think people should try and help women, not just send them to prison. Women have much more problems – money problems, all sorts of problems. It's not a good place, prison. People should be given opportunities to see whether they can change. Not locked up twenty-four hours a day.

Since we spoke to Adaku she has moved away. We have not been able to trace her.

Jean

Jean was aged thirty-seven when we saw her. She was a single parent and had a nine-year-old son, Darren, who was in a home for mentally handicapped children. With a long history of severe depression and alcoholism, Jean was arrested for arson and spent seven months on remand on C1, the psychiatric unit of Holloway prison. At the time we saw her, Jean was living in a hostel in North London and attending a psychiatric day centre.

At any one time there are a significant number of women who are particularly distressed and disturbed serving prison sentences, mostly for very trivial offences. Many are kept in prison for several weeks, sometimes months, as was the case for Jean, whilst psychiatric and medical reports are prepared for the courts. Holloway prison's C1 unit has for some time been the subject of public concern and outrage. Situated on the ground floor of the prison, it is dark, depressing and claustrophobic. It is staffed by prison officers and nurses and the discipline and medical roles often conflict. It operates on the same lines as the rest of the prison, with the same rules and system of privileges and punishments. Whilst Jean was there, the women were spending anything up to twenty-three hours a day locked in their cells. Self-mutilation is not uncommon on the wing. Women have, in their distress, been known repeatedly to bang their heads on the walls and floor to cut and injure themselves. In 1984 there was considerable publicity concerning a woman who gouged out her eye and another who slashed her breast in order to get out of her cell for a few minutes. Since then, there has been continual pressure from ex-prisoners and from penal reform and mental health organisations for the closure of the wing.

Whilst Jean was a prisoner on C1, Marc Sancto (born Anne Franklin) a female transsexual, died there in December 1985. The coroner's verdict was 'Accidental death due to lack of care'.

I am what is commonly known as a loner. I was born in Buckinghamshire, my father was a farm worker, so we moved round quite a bit. I went to eleven different schools. I've got two sisters: one's disappeared, the other's married. Both my parents are dead. Mum died in '74, two weeks after Terry, my first boy, was born. Dad died a few years before that – I'm not sure when.

I was antagonised a lot when I was little. The boys at school used to make fun of me because I have a crooked spine. The older girls used to stand me in a corner of the playground and throw stones at me. I stopped going to school when I was thirteen getting on fourteen, and it was then that I started getting into trouble, running away from home and thieving. I was considered out of care and control. I had a dirty great chip on my shoulder. I thought everybody was against me and I didn't feel loved by anybody. I couldn't make friends so I went around by myself, did things by myself.

It was when I was fifteen or sixteen that I committed my first big offence. I committed arson. I set fire to a barn, not realising that there was a sick cow in there that perished, and I got three years' approved school. I found the school hard at first because I hated being shut in. I ran away two or three times, but each time I got brought back.

I made a friend, though. Her name was Doris and I settled down and ended up working in the kitchen which I enjoyed. When I was eighteen and a half I was let out, but I think I got institutionalised being there three and a half years, and I wanted to stay there. I felt safe. But I was sent back home anyway. Mum was given a choice: either to stay in the caravan they were living in and not have me home, or move into a flat so I could live with them. So my Mum had to move into a flat. She blamed me for that.

I went to the flat and I got myself a job working in Woolworth's in Reading. It was then I started making hoax calls. I used to ring up the ambulance people: 'There's a fight and somebody's got hurt at the Queen's Head.' And I wouldn't give them my name. I used to hang around until the ambulance came. It was excitement, I suppose, I just felt excited by it. One time, though, they caught me. It was then I had my first taste of prison. I spent three days in Holloway on remand. I got out on bail, I think it was my probation officer who rang up. He said I should never have been sent there. I ended up on three years' probation. I settled down again with my Mum and Dad. We moved to another flat and then to a maisonette on the same estate. Then Mum had cancer and Dad was taken ill at work. After some time he died, coronary thrombosis.

Although I used to enjoy a drink, I started really drinking heavily after he died. I loved my father, and when he died I felt something I loved had been taken away from me. A little while after that my Mum went to live with my sister and her family, so I had to go into a bedsit. I'd go out, go to the social club, have a few drinks. I'd almost always be on my own. Occasionally I'd meet up with others, but not often. I didn't get difficult when I drank but I often couldn't remember where I'd been or what I'd done or even how I'd got back home. I managed to stay out of trouble, though.

In 1974 my first boy was born. I wanted the baby. I was on the pill at the time, but I deliberately left it off because I wanted someone to love. Two weeks after Terry was born, my Mum died of cancer. It was expected. It didn't hurt so much as it did with my Dad passing away. Anyway, I looked after Terry for two and a half years. He was born with a heart complaint, and in November '76 he went up to Hammersmith Hospital, and on 2 December he had an operation. He pulled through, but then his kidneys failed and he died. Although I'd rung on the Thursday and they said his kidneys were failing, it still came as a shock when they rang on the Saturday at 9.30 in the morning to say he'd died.

Then I really started drinking heavily. I knew I had a drink problem. I went to my doctor and can't remember what I said to him or what he said to me, but he put me on valium. So I was drinking and taking valium. I was in a bad way at that time, I felt really depressed, so I went round causing criminal damage. I broke a window at the new police station in Reading. I threw a brick through the window, ran away and then came back and did it again. I wanted them to take me in, I wanted to get arrested. Mind you, in another way I didn't want to get arrested. I got caught and it took six policemen to hold me down. I got remanded twice, then I got probation on condition that I attended the Winterborn Unit, a mental hospital near Oxford, as a day patient. They have a coach which picked us up. I didn't like it there at first – sometimes it was traumatic, sometimes it was boring – but I wanted help, especially with my drink problem. I didn't get a lot of help from them.

Then I fell for Darren, my second son. I left the unit in '78 because I was so big with him. I couldn't stand the journey. After Darren was born, he had to stay in hospital an extra ten days because he suffered from epileptic fits. For the first two and a half years of his life he was in and out of hospital until they found the right medication. Then there was a six months period without fits and everything was going fine, and then he started up again. He had them one after another after another. I found it quite frightening. I moved again to Whitley near Reading. I stayed there for five years and was still drinking. I knew I had a drink problem – even my sister said I was an alcoholic. Then I contracted hepatitis, through drink, and my son went to a special hospital for mentally handicapped children. My sister looked after me for a week. I managed to stop drinking for four months: I kept a bottle in the house but I never touched it. I just looked at it and then shut the door. I wasn't even tempted, until Darren came home for a while and started having a lot of fits. One night I was up all night with him and I started back on the bottle. It was partly that, and partly through boredom and loneliness. I didn't really want it. Darren started going to a special school, but in '84 my drinking did start getting out of hand and I was pushing Darren from pillar to post. It was in

October of that year that I got into trouble again, the first time since '78.

They classed it as attempted robbery, because I never hurt anybody. I tried to hold this woman up in a car park underneath the council offices. I'd gone into Woolworth's in Reading and stolen a couple of things from there, and I was hanging around the car park. I saw this woman, and she looked well off. I didn't really need the money but I tried to hold her up. She told me not to be silly and went and reported me. Then I gave the police a run around the car park. Mind you, I was quite belligerent, but I wasn't violent. Also, before I did that I'd made a hoax call saying that Boots' chemist was on fire. I got charged with that and the attempted theft. I got remanded to Holloway, which I didn't like.

When I first went in, it felt strange. Going through reception they have to check everything you're bringing in, what money you have, or what have you. Then they frisk you and give you a dressing-gown and tell you to go into a cubicle and strip off and wait. I had to wait a long time shut in. It was a few feet by a few feet with a bench to sit on. After that you go into a big room and they look through your clothes and they ask you questions, then you have to pull your knickers down to your knees and do a twizzle, twist round, pull your pants up and put your dressing-gown back on. There were several officers, you felt every eye was on you. It's humiliating, degrading, having different women seeing you; I can't stand that. Then you have a bath and they give you a towel and soap. If you haven't seen the doctor before you have your bath you have to stay undressed until you have, and then he takes a few details. I told him I was an alcoholic. I was put on Heminephrin – it helps to stop the shakes and the sweats. It helps a bit, but it makes you tired. I was also on vitamin injections, because alcohol takes the vitamins out of your body.

First of all I was put in a two-person cell with bunk beds. I shared it with a coloured girl who I got on with and we had a good laugh. And then she went and another one came who was very offish. Anyway, one day I was messing about playing hide and seek, hiding from the officers, and they put me on report. The following morning at eight o'clock they said, 'You're on report, strip your bed, get your things together.' I said, 'What?' I was shocked. I was marched down to A block [punishment]. I was on at the time, I had my period. They said, 'Strip off and pull your pants down.' I said, 'I can't because I'm on.' They said, 'We'll give you a clean sanitary towel.' So they took the dirty one. Then they let me get dressed, gave me a pair of slippers, because we weren't allowed to wear shoes, and said I had to wait to see the Governess. I saw her and she said fourteen days' loss of privileges. I tried to speak. I tried to explain. I started moving forward, so the screws started closing in on me. I felt really claustrophobic. I was going to lash out, I wanted to strangle her, I was really getting uptight and my head was spinning. I was taken back to the cell, where I started throwing the furniture about. I was crying. I thought fourteen days was a ridiculous sentence just for messing about. I was just having a game. They turned round and said I was wasting the officers' time, looking around searching for me, but I couldn't go anywhere with all the doors locked.

Eventually, I was taken back up to my wing. The officer who took me back, she's a right bitch. She said, 'Come on, get your stuff together, you're going.' So I went like a little lamb following a mother sheep, back to the same room. In the end I got moved into a single cell: apparently a lot of this girl's stuff went missing and she practically accused me. I never took it. Anyway, it was better being in a cell on my own. I was in prison on remand for three weeks, then I went to court and got three years' probation.

I went back home to Burford and settled in. Darren was in this privately run home for mentally handicapped children near Basingstoke. After Christmas, in February, I was allowed to go and see him. I wanted him to be home with me, but I needed to get myself sorted out. Things, though, went from bad to worse, and the following January I tried to commit suicide because I felt I couldn't go on. I had a bottle of VP Rich Ruby wine, and Darren's tablets were in the house, and I had some pain killers.

I took all of them, then I phoned up a couple of people I knew. How I managed to do that I do not know. They got in touch with my sister, who got in touch with Mortimer police – I can't remember letting them in. I had to keep walking round and round and I wanted to go to sleep. They took me to the hospital, and then took me back home. After that I tried to settle down. I tried the AA; that didn't work. The probation found a little stray dog called Benjy for me and I looked after him for a little while, but my money kept on going down and down and down. Social security were paying my bills for me, but the more they paid the more they took off me. I had to try and live on less than £18 a week. In the end I had to let Benjy go because I couldn't afford the dog food. That was something else that was taken away from me. I had Darren home for weekends once a month. Things started working out a bit better, but towards the end of '85 everything started getting too much; the pressures, trying to pay my bills and trying to get extra money in. I wasn't drinking an awful lot so I decided that even with the difficulties I was going to have Darren home for good. I thought I could cope, but deep down a little nagging voice said to me, leave him where he is, he's happy, he's settled, have him home for the holiday. But I felt I'd let him down. I'd said I wanted him back, but I was frightened and I felt I couldn't face telling the social workers.

In October, on 3 October 1985, I was feeling so depressed I thought the walls were caving in on me. I wanted to stay in but I wanted to go out, and vice versa. Latish that night I got a box of matches and my torch and went across the back field and set fire to this Dutch barn. I didn't think it had ignited and I was walking away from it when all of a sudden I heard all this crackling and banging. I was half way up the road when I saw the fire engine come. This woman said to me, 'See the fire engine?' and I said, 'What fire engine? I don't live round here', and my mind sort of blacked out and I can't remember getting home, though I did get back, changed my clothes and had a bath. I thought I was cracking up. I didn't feel nothing: I didn't feel remorse, I didn't feel guilty, I felt as though my mind and body were dead inside. Then I phoned up the police – I phoned them up two or three times – and told them I'd done it, but they wouldn't believe me. In the end they said they'd come round. I went out for a walk because I couldn't stand being indoors. When I came back they were waiting for me. They asked me a few questions and they said, 'You'd better come along to the police station.' They took away my jacket and trousers, which I was going to wash, and also my shoes. I didn't have any others so I went to the police station in stocking feet. At the police station, they kept on asking me questions until the early hours of the morning, but they were nice and I was allowed to phone my solicitor. On 4 October 1985 I was charged with arson.

I ended up in Holloway. Again I went through the same reception, being sort of frisked, getting undressed, doing a twizzle, seeing the doctor, having a bath. As soon as they realised my charge was arson I was left to sit in the cubicle: everybody else disappeared. They went up to their separate wings and I was left to last. I ended up on D1 [the reception wing] and stayed there until Saturday afternoon. Then a nurse and officer came and said, 'Come along, dear, we're taking you to another wing.' They took me along and they put me into this dormitory. It wasn't until half an hour later that I realised I was on C1. I just felt dead. I was sleeping most of the time, I didn't want to eat, I wasn't hungry. Then I was put on some sort of medication to help me calm down because I kept on getting knotted up, getting uptight. All I wanted to do was throw things, get this feeling out of me. I felt like smashing up. The doctor who gave me the medication asked me, 'Why did you do it?' and I couldn't answer because I didn't know. A lot of things just didn't sink in.

When I was there I heard a lot of screaming and banging. People would yell or shout out, put excreta through the door hatch or throw their dinner out. We didn't get out of the cells very often. Now and again we had association or exercise, but most of the time we were locked up twenty-two and twenty-three hours a day. Often you'd hear somebody playing up, or you heard the screws zooming around because someone had cut up [injured themselves]. I cut up once. I scratched 'Darren' on my arm with a pin. I just felt like doing it. It was when I hadn't seen him for a long time and I was all wound up.

I'd been there a few months when me and a girl called Sue and a girl called Monica started playing silly devils, throwing things out of the hatch. We done it for a laugh and because we were bored and it got out of hand. Then we barricaded ourselves in, piled our mattresses against the cell door. The screws made up promises, like if we took the barricade down they'd leave us alone, they wouldn't punish us. I knew something was going to happen because Miss [E] took off her jacket and rolled up her sleeves. I said to her 'Are you coming in?' and she said, 'No we're not.' I thought, 'You lying bitch.' It's very rare that I swear. We were shouting at them through the hatch. They did come in, and it took seven of them to get me down to a single cell. I didn't struggle a lot, but one of them pushed my head right down, my arms were pulled right back. If they had left us, things would have been all right. They didn't need to do that, charging in the way they did.

I was frogmarched down to a single cell. I was so worked up, I kept slamming my bed against the wall, banging on windows, turning the taps on. So they cut my water off. And I just kept banging my bed against the door, just to get rid of my angry, violent feelings. That night I kept on and on – bang, bang, bang. I was tired but I kept on doing it and doing it; they asked me to stop but I wouldn't. In the end they opened the door and forced their way in. Again they pushed my head right down. They said, 'Get on the floor.' I refused. I said to them, 'I won't kneel to any of you bastards.' I wouldn't, especially to them. So my head was pushed down and my arms pulled behind my back. Anyway, they dismantled the bed and I was left with a strip blanket [a sheet of heavy material designed to be almost impossible to tear] and a mattress, one heavy black mattress. After I'd quietened down they left me alone.

You're not allowed matches on C1, but you're allowed baccy. Some women can't make it last the week so theirs is kept in the office. We had one roll-up an hour and you had to roll them so thin to make the tobacco last: jaw-achers they were. Make your jaw ache drawing on them. If your cigarette went out the screws would come back and light it if they was in the right frame of mind: all depends who was on. If they didn't feel like coming back you'd have to wait till the next hour. That's when a lot of the girls started banging on the door, screaming and shouting. The only time we was allowed to smoke more was on association, but we were banged up most of the time.

When we had association we'd stand around and talk, or sit and watch telly or have a bath and wash our hair. A lot of girls just had one bath a week. They only let us out for baths if there was enough staff, otherwise you had to have a strip wash. There was no privacy, no curtain round the sink, so you had to do your top first, keep your nightdress on, wash your bottom part and hope people weren't looking. It was embarrassing. There was only one toilet and you just had to hope no one came in with any diseases or anything.

Their excuse for not letting us out more often was that there wasn't enough staff. That's lies: there *was* enough staff. We needed more freedom, more room to move. That's what made us play up, people just sitting there, not able to go up to the STU [occupational therapy] because there wasn't enough officers or staff to take us. They just couldn't be bothered half the time. After I'd been there a few months I was asked if I wanted to help out in the kitchen, which I did. I was a wing worker. I was let out between eight and half-past in the morning, locked back in at dinner time, let out to do the washing up and scrub the kitchen floor in the afternoon, and then locked up again.

First of all I thought the nursing staff was nice, but there was a couple who were right bitches. They used to wind people up. They'd stand there and laugh at you, or say things to get you going, and when they felt they'd wound you up they'd walk away laughing. A lot of *them* were slow, and didn't know what they were doing half the time: they'd give you the wrong medicine. I was offered the wrong medicine twice.

While I was in a single room, what I used to do was get hold of sani towels and put my dog ends in and let them smoulder and wave them out the hatch. And they used to say, sniff, sniff,

'What's that burning? I can smell something burning. It's coming from your room.' 'No it's not.' And then I chucked it out the window. I done that twice, and got put on report for it. This woman, an assistant governor, I think, asked me why I did it. I didn't tell her. I wrote it down. I mentioned that I missed my son and how I couldn't see him. I only saw him twice. They arranged for Darren to come up before Christmas. It was a journey I wouldn't have wished on him. I was told I could see him for an hour but they got held up on the way and I was rushed through the visit. Darren was very distressed, which hurt. I only saw him for half an hour. That choked me up. I kissed him goodbye and said, 'See you soon.' The other time I was taken to see him, which was better. I didn't have much other visitors. A neighbour came to see me twice. I was allowed to see her in the visiting room, but if some of the girls knew you were from C1 they'd call you muppet. We weren't the muppets, they were.

Whilst I was there on C1 a woman died. It gave us all a terrible shock. She/he was ever so nice but a lot of the staff and nursing staff were right bastards to him. They kept on saying to him that he could do more for himself, that he was putting a lot on. He had a bad leg and they kept on at him to hurry up. He was handicapped and I've got a handicapped son: I can't stand people who take the mickey out of those sort of people. Some of the officers kept on to him to pull himself together and that sort of thing. He was always on his own and you'd hear him crying out. I knew something had happened because the governor came down. We very rarely saw the governor – especially late afternoon or evening – and there was a lot of hustle and bustle. Then I found out he hung himself. I think he done it because he was picked on a lot and most likely thought he hadn't got a lot going for him. I felt choked, but I couldn't cry. I felt very sorry for him, but there again, the way he was and the way he felt, he's better off out of it. But they shouldn't have shut him up on his own. They could have looked after him more. He was well liked, even on the other wings. He did look mannish. He should never have been in prison. It was very upsetting.

I was also on C1 when the BBC came round to do that

programme: 'Forty Minutes', I think it was called. A lot of the staff didn't want their faces on TV or names mentioned, which was understandable. But as soon as the television come round there was a helluva change in the screws, being falsely nice. There's one kept saying, 'If there's anything wrong, dear, you know you can always come to me to talk about it.' This was in front of the cameras, and I thought, 'You two-faced bitch', because if I ever tried to talk to her she'd either be sarcastic or looked through you, looked away or didn't want to know. The only time I spoke to the cameras was when me and another woman were in the kitchen and we had to sort of make a conversation. It's quite hard really. I felt that was false. I don't think they got a true picture, especially not of C1, because the staff reacted in a helluva different way to when the cameras weren't there.

A lot of the staff were all right, but they didn't understand. They'd say, 'We're here to help you, that's what we're here for, to listen to your problems.' But then they'd say, 'I can't stand here listening to you all day', and go off and do something else. As far as I was concerned, a lot of them didn't really want to know. I wouldn't really talk to them anyway, but sometimes you needed to talk to somebody, or to sort something out. Half the time they didn't understand what you was trying to tell them, and you could feel yourself working up, through frustration.

During the seven and a half months I was on C1 I went to Crown Court twice, and each time I got remanded back into Holloway. I had a circuit judge so everywhere he went I had to follow. One night, a Wednesday, I was told that I was leaving Holloway the next day to go up to Risley remand centre because my judge was at Sheffield. When I got there they moaned about all the clothes and stuff I had, because you have to take everything with you when they move you about. At Risley, when they say 'Strip' you have to really strip: take off everything. I had a bath, then had to wait to see this officer in charge, and because they read on my notes that I'd barricaded, I was put on this wing like C1. The person that was in my cell before me had urinated in it, so I had to clear it up before I could sleep and that wasn't nice. You're lucky if you have a roll-up in Risley. They have this little peephole where you have to shove your cigarette so it sticks out on the other side for them to light it. I went to bed early: I felt numb from head to foot, didn't have no feelings.

Whilst I was in Holloway, my probation officer sorted out something to try and stop me getting a prison sentence. Someone from a hostel in London came to see me and said they would have me, so when I went to court in Sheffield the judge decided to put me on bail for four weeks, on condition that I stayed at the hostel and that I didn't drink, and also if I attended the Jules Thorn psychiatric unit, which is part of St Pancras Hospital, for a ten-day assessment. So I stayed at the hostel for four weeks. When I went to the Royal Courts of Justice, the judge knew what he was going to give me, and I got three years' probation, on condition that I stay at the hostel for a year and that I attend a day centre. I started at the Jules Thorn unit on 13 July. It's nice. I like it there. I attend different groups, and I've got a key worker who I see once a week. Most people said I should get probation, but I was looking on the black side and thought I would get a sentence of three to five years.

I've had to give my home up. The council want my flat. I'm now waiting to hear from the DHSS to see if they will spend so much money a week for storing my furniture. I can go home now and again to stay with my sister, and Newbury Council have said that when I come back into circulation they'd be willing to find me another place, and hopefully I'll find a little job. I've been told when I do get settled into my new home, maybe that I'll be able to have Darren home once a month. In the meantime I'll just carry on going to visit him. I'm not giving that up.

I don't think I could ever go back to Bedford to live, and I couldn't never live in that flat anyway because it's been desecrated. I thought the woman I left my key with, a neighbour, was a friend. But it's either her or the caretaker who've taken a lot of stuff out of my place: radio cassette, bedside radio, camera, alarm clock, my son's chair and table. I think she must have had that for her little boy. All my tools which I had underneath the kitchen sink, my washing powder: all gone. Tinned food and other stuff: disappeared. I don't know what to do about it. I don't want it to upset me. There again, I don't know whether to confront her about it, write her a letter or what. I could ask my probation officer to try and sort things out, but I know she'll deny it.

I did seven and a half months in prison: that was more than enough. I don't think I could have handled it if I'd been given a sentence. Otherwise I got on pretty well, had a laugh: you had to. I don't think a lot of the staff liked you laughing and joking about. It's not what they said, it's the looks you got from some of the screws, as if to say, 'You shouldn't be laughing, what have you got to be happy about?'

I can't see the future very clear at the moment. I've been feeling so depressed and tearful and choked up. It started coming back after a weekend seeing Darren. I didn't want to come back. I cried on Monday night and cried again Tuesday and yesterday. And today I've been feeling down. I've got to look towards the future, but I can't really see anything, not the way I feel. And this is how I started off before I got into trouble. I don't know what I want to do, besides going home. I was asked if I had ever thought about finding a flat and living up here. No way. Too much of a rat racc. I could never live in London. Rushing, rushing, traffic from morning to night: it goes on twenty-four hours a day. I like being with people, but there's times when I want to be on my own. I know if I feel depressed I shouldn't just sit on my own, you just dwell on it: 'Why did I do this, why did I do that?' I start thinking about Darren. I know he's happy where he is but I miss him. There isn't a day that goes past without my missing him. And I miss my family. I've only been out of prison three months. It takes it out of you. So I'm bound to feel a bit low, aren't I? I know if I get into trouble again I'll be done for the arson charge and breach of probation, and that means a few years in jail and I couldn't handle it.

I've learnt my lesson. I'm thirty-six years old. I've been in and out of places, I've had to learn the hard way. They couldn't make head or tail of me, couldn't think what was wrong with me. I can't remember what was the name they put on it. But I wasn't insane.

Jean's son Darren died from a major epileptic fit three months after this interview. Jean remained at the hostel and continued to attend the Jules Thorn Unit. Several months later she was arrested for climbing the scaffolding and smashing a window at the National Gallery in Trafalgar Square. At the time of going to press she is back in the C1 psychiatric unit at Holloway as a convicted remand prisoner waiting to go to court.

Sharon

When we met Sharon she was living in a London hostel for women recently released from prison. She had been out of prison for two months and was in the process of re-establishing herself in the outside world. She had one daughter, aged two and a half years, who was living with her mother.

The prison officers' dispute Sharon refers to is the Prison Officers Association overtime ban started at the end of April 1986. It was called off within twenty-four hours after extensive rioting at a number of men's prisons.

If he was to walk in here today and I knew he was my stepfather, I would not think twice about putting a knife through him. My mum is now registered blind: that's through the severe beatings to the head she had from him. My brother Sean is very slow, and I feel my stepfather had something to do with that too. I'm not using him as an excuse or anything, but I do feel he's got a lot to do with the way my life's been.

As a child I was sexually assaulted by my stepfather. That was an experience I went through for many months, not saying anything. My stepfather was saying to me, 'This is my way of showing you how much I love you and care for you.' I was only young, about eight years old. It's always been on my mind – I suppose it always will – and I've always said that if I got the opportunity to kill the man I'd do it, and I would take the consequences. He has very, very deeply scarred me.

When I became a prostitute I used to think, 'Men are paying *me*. They're not getting anything out of me, they're having to pay me for my body.' I hated them, I used to laugh at them. I really detested them, and I think my stepfather had a lot to do with that as well. Nothing ever happened to him. He never went to court because they said I was too young to give evidence. As far as I was concerned, he got away with it. The only thing that really happened was that my mum got a divorce in 1972 on the grounds that he had sexually assaulted me and there was mental cruelty to her. If I do something stupid, like if I do a chequebook and card, I go to prison. He nearly kills people and nothing happens to him. This is what I can't understand.

The relationship between me and my mother was bad because my mother suffered a nervous breakdown and everything, and she blamed her children for a lot of things that went wrong with her. My stepfather was a very violent man. If she put an ashtray in the wrong place, she'd get beaten up; if she never put his paper in the right place, she'd get beaten up; if he came in from work and his dinner wasn't on the table, she'd get beaten up. It was terrible the things that used to happen. I think it was that which made her frightened to accept the truth when he was sexually assaulting me. As a child you don't know what to do: a child should be able to trust its mother 100 per cent.

I was truanting from school when I was about nine, and to be truthful my mother said I was totally out of hand. So they took me into care and put me in an assessment centre in Sydenham Hill for six months. After that I was put with foster parents, staying with them in the country for about nine months. Then I was taken back home to my mother's and tried to build up the relationship again. By this time I was in secondary school. I never got on very well and ended up getting thrown out of my classes. As a last resort I was put into a special centre for people who won't adjust to school. One day my mum rang up and said she didn't want me to come home again and that I should go to Social Services because she was sick and tired of all the bother and everything. So I was taken into care again, went to an assessment centre and ended up in an approved school for girls in Hertfordshire.

My first offence was round about the age of eleven – shop-lifting. I think every child goes through a stage where they go into a shop and nick something: they just want to see whether they can get away with it. But that was really my first encounter with the police. When you're a child they say, 'You know you shouldn't do that', and they give you a bloody good rollicking and leave it at that – they try to terrify you. But then I started getting into trouble in approved school – running away, things like that, ending up in Brighton and Margate and being arrested for being an absconder from council care. I was always taken back. The approved school was bloody disgusting. If you got into trouble you were made to sit on a chair and look at a wall for twenty-four hours a day. You wasn't allowed to talk to anybody else. You wasn't allowed to smoke – that was one privilege they did normally let you have: if you were over fourteen you were allowed up to four cigarettes a day. If you did get in any trouble there was this man, Joe, and he was a really big hard man, he was a black-belt in karate and everything, and he really did mentally and physically terrify the girls.

One time me and my friend Yasmin, we were both in there. We used to go out on these walks in the country near the school, and we were accused of going with two lorry drivers behind a bush to have sex with them in exchange for a watch. Letters went home to our parents about it, our weekend leave was stopped and we wasn't allowed to associate with any of the other girls. They had this little room, half the size of a prison cell, and if you did anything wrong you were put in there with just a mattress, and you was left there locked in, to stew really. You had your meals brought to you – it was just disgusting. They used to beat us up, literally beat us up and terrorise us. I mean, for a child to have to sit and look at a wall for twenty-four hours a day – it's totally out of order, you know.

I used to tell my mum everything that went on, but nobody would believe us. When parents or social workers went up to see us, obviously they had to see the staff, and the woman in charge was so nice, she had this big front – 'My girls, my girls' – it was totally a load of shit. About three years ago I was reading a newspaper and there was this big article about my approved school. I don't know whether it closed down or not but there was a big inquiry into it. I was just thankful that I got out when I did. Time after time I ran away and my social worker could see that I wasn't happy. I'd made it clear that by the time I reached sixteen I wanted out – I couldn't get out any sooner because no school in London would have me. When I left there I thought it was the happiest day of my life, but it wasn't.

I couldn't go home to my mother because the relationship was still very iffy, so I ended up going to a hostel. I didn't get on very well there either. I was moved to another hostel which was worse. I had just turned sixteen and they put me in this place that was really for dossers. I couldn't stick it and they couldn't find me anywhere else, so I took off. Obviously if you're on your own, single, with nowhere to live, you have to have money and you have to get somewhere to live, so I turned to prostitution. I met this man and I thought he was wonderful – so nice to me and everything when I first met him. I thought, 'Oh my God, I've found someone at last that really does care for me.'

At first I didn't mind doing it, but after two months I found out he had quite a few women. He didn't really care for me at all: it was my money he was interested in. He started knocking me about and telling me that I had to bring in this or that amount of money. After a while I thought, 'Hold on a minute, this isn't right. I shouldn't be doing this.' I just stood up to him one day – don't ask me where I got the nerve from, because he was a bloody big geezer. I said to him, 'If you want money, go out there and fucking get it yourself. I'm nobody's slave.' He battered me – and when I say battered, I mean battered. He ended up breaking my nose, I had four broken ribs, a broken arm and my shoulder was dislocated. I went to the hospital and they asked me how I done it. Obviously you don't say, 'Oh my pimp beat me up', do you? If you did, the police would get involved, and that's the last thing anyone wants 'cause the pimps terrify you as far as the police are concerned. So I said I fell down a flight of stairs.

I still needed money so I had to carry on working the streets. I was going round in circles because it's a very small world – pimps and prostitutes. There's only a certain number of places a prostitute can go and earn money, so all a pimp needs to do is drive round in his car until he sees you. When he gets you he beats you up for leaving him; you go back and start working for him again; then you try to get away from him; he finds you again and you just go on like this all the time. I decided, 'Right this isn't it', so I left and set up on my own. By that time I'd heard my pimp was in custody, and I started renting a flat. I had to do something to keep my flat going and everything, so I got in with these girls, working girls. I said, 'If you want somewhere to use, you can use my flat, just as long as there's only one of you in there at a time.' You see, with things like that you can start getting done with living off immoral earnings, brothel-keeping and whatever, and at that age – nearly seventeen – I really didn't want those type of charges.

There was me and two other girls working in one flat. Everything was going fine for about four months. I had sorted out the flat really nicely, and had some money put away. One day one of the girls who came from Birmingham (she used to come down, work the week and go back up), she just got up and said, really unexpectedly, 'I'm going back.' So me and the other girl left that evening to go to work. I came back to the flat with one of my regular clients who I had planned to meet. I hadn't been back longer than ten minutes when I got a sledgehammer through my street door. I thought, 'My God, what's happening?' At first I thought it was some pimps, the door literally came off its hinges. Then in walked all these men. I seen one woman and she had a police uniform on, so obviously I knew it was the police. I'll always remember it. Chief Inspector [E] was there and he turned round and said, 'Sharon Mills?' and I said, 'That's right,' and he said, 'I'm charging you with running a brothel and living off immoral earnings.' So I says, 'You've got to be joking.' He said, 'No, I have statements, I have witnesses and we've been surveying you for the last four months.' I went totally mad because there was an officer there that I knew – an officer that had picked me up and everything – he had arrested me before, but had also done business with me. I felt he'd sort of taken the piss out of me, through doing business with me. He knew about them investigations, that I was being watched, and he could have told me to slow down a bit. But he never, and I went really mad. I grabbed at him and went totally berserk. I ended up getting carried to the station with my feet handcuffed, my hands handcuffed, lain in the bottom of the van. They stopped my client, asked him what he was there for, his name and address, the usual routine. The poor sod must have been terrified because he was married with children. That was the last I seen of him. They searched my whole flat before they took me, looking for things like Durex, and to see whether I kept any books of accounts, of girls giving me money, all this sort of thing. When I got to the station they read the charge against me, charged me with it and I asked whether I was getting bail. They kept me in custody overnight. I went to court the next morning, was refused bail and was remanded to Holloway. I was just seventeen.

Seven days later I went to court and still got refused bail. I went back to court seven days after that, there was a bail application put forward and the magistrate said he would grant bail with a surety of £500. So my solicitor said to me, 'Who do you know that can stand surety for £500?'. I said, 'To be quite truthful, nobody' – because I had no contact with my family. All I knew were prostitutes or pimps, and just about everyone had a criminal record. Nobody would stand surety, so bail wasn't granted again. Then I remembered someone who could: the person could not stand cash, but was maybe prepared to put something up of the value of £500. I was taken back to Holloway while they made inquiries. I thought, 'That's it – I'm not getting out, I'm staying.' It must have been about 9.30 one evening when the cell hatch opened and they said, 'Mills, you've got bail. Do you want to go now or in the morning?' I said,

'What do you mean? Let me out now!' Who's going to stay in prison longer than they have to?

The next day I went down to where I used to work. I had been to my flat and there was nothing there – it had been totally cleared out. So I wanted to see the girl I had worked with because she must have known what happened to my stuff. I was walking along the road and all of a sudden this police car drew up beside me. They said, 'Hello Sharon.' I looked and said, 'Yes?' They said, 'Would you get in the car please?' I said, 'What for?' They said, 'We're arresting you for loitering with the intent of prostitution.' I said, 'Do me a favour.' Now I'm known to the police as a 'common prostitute' – why 'common' I don't know. Prostitute – well, I can accept that, but common I will not accept. I said, 'Look, you know I've just come out of Holloway after being on remand.' They were the same officers that had arrested me for the charge I was on. 'You know I'm not working, I'm down here trying to find out where my stuff's gone to.' Anyway, this woman grabbed hold of me, and she just done it wrong. The judge who gave me bail had said that if I got into trouble that was it, I wouldn't get bail again, so obviously I thought, 'If I'm going to go back, I'll go for something worth going for.' Me and the woman police officer started fighting and then the other two men come out. I'll always remember it – I can see it and laugh about it now. It was raining and there was this walkie-talkie twisting around my head, there was police hats rolling in the road, and they radioed in for assistance. There must have been about nine or ten of them – all men except for one woman – and they tried to say it took all of them to restrain me. Now I was a lot skinnier then than I am now, about seven and a half stone, and they tried to say that! They had handcuffs on me and I've still got marks on my hands – you can see – where the handcuffs were put on so tight that when I got to the station they couldn't get them off me.

I was back in court the next day and I ended up getting twelve months for GBH [grievous bodily harm] on a police officer. I think it should have been the other way round because I was black and blue from head to toe. When I got into Holloway they have them little forms and they've got pictures of a body with all arrows and everything, and where I had any bruises the doctor put these marks. It was like from head to toe there was these marks on my body where I had bruises, and *I* got done for *police assault* – I couldn't believe it! While I was doing that sentence my other case for running a brothel and living off immoral earnings came up. I was only in court for about fifteen minutes and the judge dismissed the case for lack of evidence. It was all for nothing.

I did both my sentences at Cookham Wood: I was only on remand at Holloway. I will never understand why I went to Cookham on my first sentence – I got a YP [young prisoner's sentence] and don't know why I never went to borstal – they still had them then. I was the youngest prisoner ever to go to Cookham Wood: now they don't take anyone under twenty-one. Going to a new prison, you don't know what to expect. Walking along the corridor, there are all these eyes looking at you, and you think, 'Oh my God.' For someone to understand the way you feel when you go into any prison you'd have to experience it. When I went into prison I had mixed feelings for people outside – I hated them, I felt they had rejected me, they'd left me alone to just get on with it. 'Not to worry, she's only got a short sentence, she'll be out soon': that's what people were saying. I can remember being in a cell, locked in, with nobody else but myself, crying, and a screw opening the hatch on the door and saying, 'What's the matter with you? You're in here because you did wrong, no tears are going to help you.' I did nine months of that sentence.

If you come out to nothing like I did and you've been a prostitute and know it's easy money – well you're going to go straight to it again. I started working straight away *and* started getting arrested – I mean, not once: I was getting arrested three times a day. Once I got arrested one morning for soliciting, but they let me out of the police station; I got arrested the same afternoon, they let me out again; I got arrested in the evening and they kept me in and took me to court the next day. I got a £50 fine. Then I thought, 'Well, blow this.' I wasn't really getting anywhere, so I started doing chequebooks and cards (amongst other things). The first time I got charged with chequebooks and cards I got two years' probation. I mean, I've had totally everything you can get from a court. I've had probation, conditional discharge, deferred sentences, suspended sentences – everything.

I think I was about nineteen when I started taking drugs. I got caught with all these drugs in a car by the same police (I don't know what I do, but it's the same police every time I get arrested) and I got charged with possession. They had to go away to be analysed, and I went back to court and ended up getting a £150 fine or seven days in prison – I paid the fine. Some people would say they'd do the seven days, but I don't like prison. I think I took drugs to escape my problems, because I thought I had the world on my shoulders for a number of reasons. I had recently had my little girl, her dad had walked out on me, and I thought he was just another man who had what he wanted and then left me. I had a house to maintain, my daughter and no job. They expected me to live on supplementary benefit so I was having to work the street, trying to get my house together.

I started off smoking hash; from that I went to acid, LSD, speed, things like that. Then I started dabbling in cocaine. I'd seen somebody taking it so I tried it and liked it. I obviously wanted some more but it was very expensive: coke sells for between £80 and £120 per gram, and a gram's not a lot at all. So, I was back working the streets to buy my drugs. Before I knew it, I was very very bad on it. For example – I feel disgusted and ashamed – I took my little girl down to my mum's and I swear to God I remember dressing her – it was winter – but when she got to my mum's house I took her out of the buggy and all she had on was her nappy and her socks and a blanket wrapped round her. I've never done anything to hurt my little girl, I've never hit her or anything like that, but I felt in myself that her being with me was endangering her. I just couldn't cope with myself, let alone her. I reached the stage where I didn't do the washing or the washing up, I didn't clean the house: it looked like a pigsty. Then I lost all pride in my appearance: I stopped changing my clothes, I stopped washing. People that knew me were asking what was wrong with me, they were shocked at the state of me. I had some arguments: 'Who do you think you are, trying to bring me down?'

One day my mum said to me, 'You're going to be in trouble before long.' I said, 'What are you talking about? You're always throwing in my face that I'm going to get in trouble. Every minute of the day, all I hear is that I'm going to get in trouble.' 'Just mark my words, Sharon,' she says, 'within six months you'll be in prison again.' I thought, 'Fuck it, she don't even know what she's talking about.' One day I was out working the streets, I went with this punter and I went back to his place. I ended up having a fight with him, he broke my arm and I got hit on the head. I was kept in hospital overnight and then I discharged myself. My little girl Natasha was with a friend at the time and because my mum hadn't seen me for some time she was concerned. My mum knows I'm a prostitute, I was very straight with her about it. I can't say she was pleased or overjoyed, but she said, 'You're at the age where I can't tell you not to do it.' I rang my mum and she wanted to know where I was and where Natasha was. I told her I was in hospital and why. She said she had something to tell me when I got home.

When I got back, my daughter was at my mother's and my mother said that I should be ashamed of myself because Natasha had been filthy and starving hungry. I said, 'Don't give me that. I know where she was and I know the woman looks after her well.' I paid my friend for having her. I told her that what she said was a load of bollocks, and one thing led to another and my mum told me she wasn't allowing me to take Natasha with me. Natasha's father was there and was siding with my mother, saying how I couldn't take Natasha, I was an unfit mother and how he was going to get me done. He said, 'You aren't fit to have the child, you only know how to look after yourself. You spend your time whoring and getting money.' I was going mad: my mum was swearing at me, I was swearing at her; finally I just lost my temper and said, 'Right, you've got everything else.

Everything I've loved, everything I've ever wanted in life you've taken away from me, so you have Natasha. You keep her.' I said, 'I hope you'll all be fucking happy', and I walked out. I was very upset. I wanted to see Natasha, but my mother said 'No' and threatened to call in the police. I couldn't afford to get in bother with the police, so I didn't see her.

I was really hard on drugs. I was doing chequebooks and cards, and I had a very good run on them for about four months, but what with taking drugs and that I collapsed one time when I was working out on the street. I was rushed into hospital – I'd OD'd [overdosed]. When I came out, I never had a care in the world. I thought, 'Well, I haven't got my daughter, so why the fuck should I bother?' I got to the stage where I just thought, well, something's got to happen, you know? It was either OD, suicide, or something else. Then one day – I'll always remember – I was staying at a friend's house and I was sweeping this carpet and I had this vision. I seen myself and two police officers. It was really weird, it frightened me, in fact. I looked at my friend and I said, 'I'm going to get arrested today.' My friend looked at me and said, 'Don't be so bloody stupid', but I knew I was right. She said, 'Well don't go out then.' Me being Miss Know-it-all did go out, and lo and behold I got arrested. They kept me in the police station for two weeks: nobody knew where I was, not even my solicitor. I was withdrawing from drugs and in a terrible state.

After two weeks they had enough evidence and they charged me. I had eighty-nine charges and forty-four more taken into consideration, so there was a hell of a lot involved. I think the amount of money came to about £42,000 worth of fraud and deception. I went to court and was remanded into custody. I tried for bail time and time again, but it just wasn't on. By this time my mother and me were getting on just a little bit better. She was prepared to stand surety for me, but they just wasn't having it. She was at court every time with me, and she came and visited me at Holloway. I must admit that even though we don't get on – I mean, we still have our ups and downs – all through my remand and prison sentence she visited me. She made sure I had money in prison, she made sure that everything I needed I had.

I was on remand for twenty-two weeks. My solicitor told me to expect at least four years because of my previous convictions: I've got deception, deception, fraud, grievous bodily harm, assault, malicious wounding, drugs, deception and then again deception. I had literally had everything possible that a judge can give you. So I knew I was going away this time. There was no way I was going to walk out at the end of all that. But I also had charges that was nothing to do with me. When I actually got to court there was more charges than there should have been. There was no point in saying they were nothing to do with me, because I'd got so many – just over a hundred charges of fraud and deception. Who was going to believe me if I said ten of those weren't mine? Nobody, really, were they? And it wouldn't have made no difference to my sentence anyway, so what was the point? I mean, if the police can get the paperwork through the likes of me, why not? I ended up with a two-year prison sentence with another nine months suspended. So I suppose I was lucky.

Going through prison – it's an experience. It's as if you go back into your childhood again. Everyone is treated like children, it's unbelievable: everybody, young girls, old women, the whole prison. It's one big approved school, that's what it's like. I mean, there's so much that goes on in prison that people don't know about, which they should. It's the humiliation they make you feel. You go to prison for something you've done wrong, that's your punishment, but they don't need to humiliate you in the way they do.

The way they treat women with drug problems in prison is disgusting. If I was outside I would have got a lot better treatment. I went through the reception, and I was shaking; I mean I didn't need to tell them I was on drugs, they could tell the drugs were on me. When I finally saw the doctor and I said, 'Can I have something?' he said, 'What for?' I said, 'Are you blind or just stupid? I'm a cocaine addict and I need something, 'cause I've not had none for so many hours now. When I was in police custody the doctor came in to see me and gave me some tablets and I'm asking you for some now.' 'Oh yes, I suppose so', he said, and he gave me some tablets. I was on tablets for two days and then taken off, just like that. They were sleeping tablets to help me sleep. I was getting DF118s – painkillers – but they knock you out at the same time. You're like a zombie, to tell the truth. No, a drug addict doesn't get any help. The only one who spoke to me about it was a police officer when I was in the police station: 'Why is a young girl like you destroying yourself on this stuff.' I said, 'Oh for Chris'sakes, shut up – I know you're trying to be nice to me and help me, but please don't because you're just giving me a headache.'

Suicide and self-injury is an everyday occurrence in prison. You can never say who is going to try it and who isn't – I mean, I even tried it myself. People would look at me and think, 'No, she's not the type, she would never try to top herself', but I tried to do it when I was in Cookham Wood. I never saw my daughter Natasha all the time I was in prison. I had her made a ward of court to my mum because the social services – they are terrible people. As soon as they knew I was in prison they were trying to get involved and everything. The last thing I wanted on my mind was my daughter being taken into care. One day the screw came up and told me I had a visit down in the solicitor's; I went down and this man presented himself as a court welfare officer. 'I've got to write a report on you and your daughter, how your relationship is,' he said. I said, 'How are you expected to do a report?' This was March and I wasn't due out until August. He said, 'I want to bring your daughter up to the prison.' I said, 'On your bike! She's not coming up to the prison, it's as simple as that.' So he said I was being very stubborn and that I'd be lucky to get my daughter back through drug addiction and one thing and another. So I told him he'd better go, because by this time I was bubbling a bit and I wanted to kill the man: I wasn't really prepared to lose any time over hitting a court welfare officer. As I was going up to my cell it all hit me – am I ever going to get my daughter back? I couldn't get out to go and see the people and ask questions, see my solicitor or anything. All I could do was write a letter, and by the time I'd written a letter and it got where it was going and a reply got back, a week or two weeks could have gone by. So I got very, very depressed about it all and I just said to the officers, 'Put me in my cell and leave me alone.' They brought the nurse round because they'd never seen me like this before. The nurse came down and gave me some medicine which totally knocked me out. I woke up in the early hours of the morning and it was still there – the first thing that come into my head. I had pictures of my little girl in the cell. Before I knew what I was doing I was slitting my wrists.

It's very frustrating being in prison. I think it's more so for women than for men. The majority of women have children, homes, financial commitments. I don't know how many people know this, but if you're in custody and you have council accommodation, the council will only pay your rent up to a year. So where does that leave a woman that gets a two-, three-, or four-year sentence? I lost my flat and practically all my belongings. Everyone's worried: am I going to get squatters? Am I going to get burgled? Are they going to take my flat away from me? Am I going to have to live on the street when I get out? What's happening to my little girl? She's growing up and I'm not there. I thought it was the most important time in Natasha's life and I wasn't there. At the same time, I was refusing for her to be brought to the prison because although I wanted to see her more than anything, I was damn sure she wasn't going to come to prison and see me. I think those types of things stick in children's minds, so I didn't want her there. It's really frustrating, all the problems you have.

When I cut my wrists it was night and I made no attempt to get the staff. I'm just lucky really that I never cut myself to any extent, because if I had tried to ring my bell, they would have said, 'Tough, wait until the morning.' That's how it is in prison. Every prison is the same, or every prison I've been in anyway. Once the door's been locked at night and the medicine's been round, you're not out until the morning. It's as simple as that.

Only a prisoner and the nurse had spoken to me the night before I cut myself. The nurse was lovely, Sister [E], practically every woman that has problems will go to her. You can sit down and talk to her; you can say anything, and no matter what you say, it's confidential between you and her. She's not going to sit down and laugh and joke over you with anyone else. I've seen a woman talking to an officer and then overheard officers discussing what she's said. As far as I'm concerned it's not on – if a woman's got a problem and she confides in you, that is a trust that shouldn't be broken. The sister was okay, you could sit and talk to her. Obviously the officers had to be told what I'd done, because injury forms and everything had to be filled in. They asked me why I tried to do it – whether I was attention-seeking! I said, 'You small-minded people make me fucking sick. Every time anyone tries to do something to themselves it's "attention-seeking". You don't stop to realise the problems women have got.' They just say, 'Well you should think of those things before you get into trouble. If you thought anything of your children you wouldn't get into trouble.' It's the same story – everyone falls back on it. So you just don't bother with them. Fuck them. I was patched up, had to see the doctor, was given some tablets and that was it. Nothing more said. My mum come up to see me and asked me what the bandage was for and I told her I'd burnt myself. She's not stupid. She knew. She told me when I come out of prison. She asked me why I tried to commit suicide. She'd come every two weeks to see me, she used to tell me everything that was going on with Natasha, and we built a very strong relationship up. I hope it will continue. We got over quite a lot of old problems.

Being close to people in prison and being close to people on the street outside are two completely different things. The people in prison are the only people you have – whatever problems you've got, you know the only people you can talk to are the women in prison. So obviously that throws you closer. And there's a lot of women in the same situation as you, what with children and one thing and another, so you discuss it and you find you're not the only one in there with those problems – there are others the same. If you're close to another woman – I'm bisexual – you can't let anyone else see that, for the fear of being split up. They victimise you if they know two women are going together; they really play on it. I don't know why they do it, the screws, because half of them are bent as butchers' hooks anyway. In Cookham Wood, especially, there are so many lesbian officers it's not true. You just have to look at them and you can tell.

I was particularly close to one girl in there, very close indeed, and we were having a relationship during the sentence I've just finished. They really did pick on her and the only reason was that she wouldn't stick up for herself. What they said went, and I'm sorry but while I was there they weren't going to get away with that. This resulted in fights and arguments – I was put on report so many times you wouldn't believe it. I had reports for disobeying orders, getting involved, stopping an officer doing what she should be doing, just through sticking up for my girlfriend. They used to see us and say, 'Here they are, the lovebirds, are we talking today or have we had a lovers' tiff?' If I was in a bad mood or something and I wanted to be on my own it would be, 'Ah, have you had an argument with the girlfriend? Is that what it is?' Or if I was to see the doctor and my girlfriend happened to be seeing the doctor as well, this was just an excuse, according to them, for us to be together. We weren't hurting anyone or upsetting anyone, it wasn't as if we stood in the corridor kissing and cuddling. Whatever we did, we did in private. It was all really stupid. So one day my girlfriend just had enough and told them to fuck off. The next day I was told to pack my stuff up because I was going on the other side [to another wing]. I was told I was getting a direct order, but I refused to pack and asked to see the governor. I was told I couldn't, but I knew if I didn't obey the order I would be put on report and would see the governor anyway. So I ended up going on report. My girlfriend was going mad and I went in front of the governor. He said to me that he doesn't agree with lesbians, thinks they are absolutely disgusting people, etc., and how two women can find sexual satisfaction with each other he will never know. I said, 'I'm not being disrespectful, sir, but it's mainly men that turn women to seek their affection from women.' He just looked at me. He said he would leave me on the wing as long as me and my girlfriend didn't twos-up with each other [visit one another's cells during the association period].

There's bent officers in there, but they think the lesbians are disgusting. How one lesbian can put another lesbian on report I will never know, because as far as I'm concerned that's hypocritical, totally and utterly. I think they should just leave women if they're having a relationship, as long as they don't interfere with anybody else. Women doing long sentences are obviously going to try and find someone to be close to. Everyone thinks lesbians are only in prison, but I know loads of women from the outside who haven't even been to prison who are lesbians. People also seem to get this impression that if you're released from prison the first thing you want is sex. Well, sex was the last thing on my mind when I got out. I didn't need it. I was getting it while I was in there, so it didn't really bother me. I had more important things to do than jump into bed with someone. But that's the impression people get: that you're like a dog on heat when you're released. It's not true.

Women who have done things to children get a bad time inside if the other women know and can get hold of them. It's the same in every prison, men's or women's. Anything you do is accepted as long as it's not interfering with children. It's just the way it's been for years. You can imagine what it's like with a 140 other women all against them. As they walk down the landing all you hear is, 'Nonce, nonce, nonce, nonce.' I've done it myself 'cause I don't like people who hurt children. But I must admit I really had a go at one nonce and felt so guilty afterwards, after she explained to me what had happened. And ever since then I've thought, 'Well, you don't know the situation, circumstances or anything, so who am I to say anything about that person? They could think what I done was totally out of order. I mean it was only forgery, but they could think it was, you know . . . They could of looked on it that I was depriving somebody. I mean the chequebooks I was doing, they could have had children couldn't they, those people? I don't know whose chequebooks I had.

Whilst I was there, there was the prison officers' dispute and the governor came into the dining room one breakfast-time and said, 'I'm sorry, girls, but there will be no visits this weekend due to lack of staff.' What governor in his right mind is going to go into a dining room of 150 prisoners and say that? You don't do that! I mean there was total chaos. I don't know how no one never got killed. Someone, I don't remember who it was, said, 'What do you mean we're having no visits?' and then everyone was off. All the doors were locked, all the prison officers were inside, and there were plates going here and plates going there and everything just went off. We all got locked in our rooms afterwards and allowed out for meals three at a time. It took them from breakfast to dinnertime to teatime to get everybody. It was really pointless. Three of you are unlocked and you come down and there are prison officers standing everywhere – to me that was stupid, because if the women wanted to riot they would have done it in the dining hall there and then. Obviously the only connections women or men in prison have are their letters and their visits. That's the only thing anyone has in prison, the only thing they have to look forward to. So to bloody tell 150 women, 'Oh, I'm sorry, but you're not having your visits' – you're asking for trouble. There wasn't any violence between prisoners in the dining hall – it was mainly smashing up prison property – but there was some violence towards the officers. There was always violence towards officers in Cookham: it happened all the time. The only way they dealt with it was to throw people down the punishment block.

It's really hard to explain how it feels to be locked in a cell. Someone has to experience it to know to the full how you feel. I'll explain what I used to do, locked up in my cell. You sit there, then you get up and you walk to one end of your cell, which isn't very far, stand there for a little while, then you walk back, look out the window, and all the thoughts go through your mind – I could be out there, your children, friends, what you'd be doing if you was out there. It's really depressing and you've got to stop thinking about it, 'cause if you don't then the emotions will come and you start crying, and you sort of think to yourself, 'No I've got to stop thinking, I've got to do something.' So you have a wash, and when you've had your wash you do a bit of your clothes washing, like your knickers and bra, then you tidy up your cell. You've done it a thousand times already, but you do it again, just for something to do. Then you start reading a book, but you can't get into it, so you get up and you tidy your cell again, and you read the book again, tidy your cell again, you know, just to keep your mind occupied because if you don't . . . I can't put it into words.

I don't know how lifers cope with it, but they do. Myra Hindley has been in prison for my whole life: I'm twenty-two now and she's been in for twenty-two years. I don't know if she'll ever get out. While I was in Cookham she got knocked back on her parole, she got a five-year review. Other people have got out and they've done similar things to her. It was so long ago that it happened – it's an everyday occurrence now, people battering and killing children. To talk to her you wouldn't believe what she'd done. She'll talk to you and give you advice and say, 'Now behave yourself, don't get into no trouble.' You wouldn't believe it. She's had some pastings while she's been away. Terrible. The way the newspapers keep writing about her just brings it all back into people's minds. Just as everyone's forgetting about Myra Hindley, there's something in the newspaper again about her.

I keep in touch with some people who are still inside – most of the people that were in with me are still there. But I met one girl by accident when I walked into the hostel one night and she was visiting another girl there. The other girl said, 'Meet my friend, this is Sophie.' She didn't recognise me. I said, 'I don't believe it', and she looked and said, 'My God, it's you, isn't it?' and I said, 'Yes it's me, Sharon.' We sat down and spoke about things that had happened. We had a good laugh, and the warmth that was there when I was in prison was still there – do you know what I mean? Nothing was different. It was as if we hadn't even parted really. I hadn't seen her since when we were on remand, and then we both got sentenced and got sent to different prisons, so I hadn't seen her for nearly a year. It was just like we were back in the cell, sitting down, having a chat and a roll-up. This time we were sitting there drinking wine and having straights [packet cigarettes]. That was quite nice, to see somebody that I'd been in prison with and still be able to sit down and talk the same old way.

I applied for parole, and usually you get your answer a couple of weeks before the date you could be going out. When you're waiting for parole you go all funny – it's like having a baby all over again. When I heard I'd got it, I was stunned – I didn't think I'd got it. But I was told about it the night before I was released! We was out on association that night and I just walked around saying, 'I've got my parole.' Everyone thought I was mucking about. I kept saying, 'Well, I've got to say goodbye, I'm going home tomorrow', and they said, 'Shut up, you're mad.' I persisted and persisted and nobody believed me. The next day came and I was running round the wing like a mad thing, up and down the stairs saying goodbye to everyone, and people were saying, 'The bastard, she's got her parole.' And I went out and that was that. Never to be seen again, hopefully. I'd still be in now without my parole – I wasn't due for release until the thirteenth of this month. I'd be counting the days now, if I hadn't got parole. My parole finishes in nine days and then I start a nine months' suspended sentence.

As for coming out: you are very wary. I always think that if someone tries to get close to me they must want something from me. My immediate reaction, whether it be a man or a woman, is to think the worst of them. They might be the nicest person, but prison has made me that way. I am very, very wary of people. I don't trust anyone as far as I could throw them: it's as simple as that.

I don't think prison really teaches you anything, though it has made me realise I'm as good as any prison officer, if not better. They always throw at you, 'You're no good', and they don't give a woman any encouragement when she's coming out. The day before I was released it was, 'Oh well, see you when you come back', not 'Good luck, don't come back.' Because I'd done two prison sentences they obviously expected me to go back again. They give you a complex about yourself. The attitude they have towards you is terrible, like you're lower than the dirt they tread on. My mother told me when I come out of prison that I'm very paranoid. Well, I don't blame any woman being paranoid when she comes out. If a woman wasn't paranoid I'd think there was something wrong with her.

But one thing prison's taught me is to be very strong, and that I *am* a worthwhile person. Nobody likes to have their freedom taken away from them, but all the abuse and everything they threw at me – it just made me stronger each time. It made me sit down and think, 'I don't give a damn what they're saying. I know I've got a life out there and I know there are people out there that care for me. I know that when I get out I'll make something of myself this time.' Obviously I can't do anything dramatic overnight, due to circumstances, what with my little girl being a ward of court, and me not having a home. But in time I'll have a home, my daughter will be back with me, and I'll be able to live as normal a life as anyone else. That is my main aim at the moment.

A year later Sharon was still living at the hostel and had managed to stay clear of drugs. She was looking forward to getting a flat of her own and was about to go to court in an attempt to regain custody of her daughter. Her main fear was that the court would regard her as an unfit mother because of her sexuality. The warden of the hostel, also a single parent, clearly had no doubts about Sharon's ability to look after children. Sharon was employed on a part-time basis to care for the warden's two-year-old daughter.

Ginger

Ginger was sentenced to three and a half years' imprisonment for illegal burial and defrauding the DHSS, and was released two years ago. She spent more than two years in Durham H Wing, the only maximum-security wing in England and Wales for women. Although there are thirty-six places on the wing, there are seldom more than three Category A women there at any one time. The numbers are made up by women who are thought to be difficult to control, like Ginger, and those who are doing medium to long sentences.

H Wing was originally used in 1961 as a special security and punishment block for male escapees, then in 1965 it was converted to take the 'Great Train Robbers' and the Kray twins. The conversion included dog runs, electronic surveillance and other security devices. In the late 1960s, hunger strikes, protests and one major riot meant the wing was rarely out of the news. Two reports were written in response to these disturbances, one by Earl Mountbatten in 1966 and the other by the Advisory Council on the Penal System in 1968. Both condemned the wing as claustrophobic and inhumane. The wing was subsequently closed, and by 1971 all the prisoners had been transferred to other prisons.

In 1974, after nearly £100,000 had been spent on new security measures, H wing was reopened for thirty-six women. Thirteen years later, despite frequent protests and lobbying on behalf of the women prisoners, it is still open.

At first you can't do anything because your mind's outside – that's your only link to sanity. In fact I had an AG [assistant governor] say to me, 'Until you get your mind into H wing you can't do your sentence.' For the first two weeks you can't adjust, you're in shock; then you start looking around and you start seeing things that are bad and people being treated badly. You start to forget about yourself and your own predicament. Maybe that's a defence. You start to kick.

I went to Durham from Risley, where I thought nothing could be worse. 'Durham's got to be better than that,' I said to myself. Getting into Durham, I thought, 'What a quaint little place – very touristy, big cathedral, little bridges, nice.' Then we got to this monstrous-looking building. It's only about two hundred yards from the centre of the town. Big gates opened, then another set of gates. I should imagine it's something like being in New York for the first time, realising how far away the sky is, how far away the light. There's no breathing space, there's monstrous ugly buildings on either side of you and they reach up for ever and there's lots of tiny, tiny little windows. You're looking all the time for a better place. After you go through the two main gates, you're driven to the bowels of the actual prison itself where H wing is. You come to this caged-off area, which has another gate. The fencing is about eighteen or twenty foot high. You get out of the vehicle escorted by two screws, who take you up to the gate. They press a button on a box and a man's voice comes over. They ask who's there. They identify themselves and say they have a prisoner. You're then told to face the camera and the gate opens. You're taken across a small concrete yard to a door and down four concrete steps. It's like entering an underground – you feel like you'll never see the light again. It's all done by voices and electronics and there's these cameras swinging at you. You look at them but you can't believe they're cameras – you think they're just pretend. You don't really believe there's anyone at the other end monitoring all this – you think it's just a sham – and there are dogs, big hefty blokes with these big dogs, and they've got radios blaring out. They press another button and they go through all the palavar again and you're thinking, 'If I go through that door, I'm never going to see the light of day again.' You think, 'This is it.' It's a desperate feeling: you're screaming inside but you don't say anything. You can't. The door opens and you get taken into a little area. From there you're taken into a little room where you're strip searched. There's no way you could have anything on you, no way, you're watched every second. I think it's to strip away your last bit of dignity. If you've got a reputation they tend to do it all the worse by saying, 'Here's a big bad one coming in', and of course the media don't help. The media reports on me in the *Sun* and the *Mirror* were gross, to say the least. In fact at one point I considered taking out an action against them. The *Mirror* was the worst.

The officers don't help you. Geordies are a strain of themselves. I've got a Geordie stepfather so I know what they're like. For a start, if you come from south of Darlington you live in an evil world, and London: 'Oh full of vice queens.' I was the only Londoner there, so you can imagine, they thought I was really bad.

It was dinnertime when I got there. There were voices coming over the loud speaker, shouting 'Food's outside' and the doors opened and these trays and big containers were brought in. [All the food for H wing is cooked by the male prisoners in the male section of Durham prison and then left outside the door of the wing to be collected. The women always worry that it has been adulterated by the men.] The smell – I can't look a mushy pea in the face now. You know that smell that lingers in hospital kitchens, that institutional smell? It doesn't matter how well a place is cleaned, it still lingers. You get a feeling of dampness there. I felt as though I was in the boiler-room of a ship – that's the only way I can describe it – a boiler-room without the noise. I was on what's known as the flat, the ground level. I looked up and you saw the suicide netting above and the landings going round where the cells are. Right up the top there's this skylight thing which is covered by wire, so hardly any daylight gets through, but everywhere's really bright with white, blazing, glaring lights. Nothing's hidden, there are no dark corners or grey areas like you get normally. Everything is on view: a little ant crawling up the wall, specks of dust – everything's exposed.

Very rarely do new people come on the wing. So my arrival was an occasion, and arriving in the middle of dinner I disorganised the routine for everyone. Their routine is so set, you can't have anything to disrupt it, it puts them all out of sync. So I suppose that got up their noses, me arriving at that time.

This other inmate was told to show me to my 'room' on the twos landing [second floor]. They call them 'rooms' – very generous of them! I was shown to this 10′ by 6′ 'room', told to make my bed and then left to my own devices. The woman who showed me asked me how long I'd got. 'Three and a half years.' 'Oh, bed and breakfast,' she said. Well of course, the majority of them are doing ten years to life: that's another thing that got up their noses. I don't blame them. Three and a half years *is* bed and breakfast. You go past the cards on the cell doors and they say 'life', 'life', 'life', 'life', and you think, 'Blimey, I've got nothing to moan about.' You start to talk to people and you say, 'How long have you got?' and they say, 'Five years' or 'Six years' or whatever and you wonder, 'Why am I here?' Even the staff ask you, 'What are you doing here if you've only got three and a half years? You must have been bad at your other prison.'

I knew three women there. Two of them were doing life. They were surprised to see me. 'What are you doing here, Ginger? I read you only got wot's it.' They want to know why, and you want to know too. I heard it was because I was a systems kicker, because of my time in Risley and at Holloway. In their terms, a difficult prisoner.

The cells on the twos landing have windows up near the ceiling, they're very high. I had to stand on the bed-head to get a glimpse of the sky. You can get put on report for that, but you couldn't see anything. Do you know what I missed? The moon. I never saw the moon the whole time I was in Durham. Everyone takes things like that for granted but when you don't see the sky, birds, normal things, animals, trees . . . Imagine not seeing a tree for five years or more. You don't know the change of seasons or anything.

The lights are on in the landings twenty-four hours a day. It's fluorescent lighting; ordinary lighting wouldn't be adequate.

The window first had plastic that could open, then you had metal grilles; beyond that you had bars and beyond that there was mesh, and then after that barbed wire. So even if the window was lower you wouldn't see much. So your only sense when you're locked in that room is your hearing. It was like being buried underground.

On the floor of the cells were grey rubberised tiles and a plastic mat. You've got your iron bed with old-fashioned wire mesh or metal slats – wire's more comfortable. There's a small wooden cupboard which has got a little drawer in, a couple of sections for jumpers and a space for hanging things. You might be lucky and get like a desk or a large bedside cupboard like you get in hospitals. You've got curtains – plain ordinary curtains with small flowers, brown, they're only on wire. You can have a bed cover but they're ever so itchy. They're made of hessian, old sacks, very rough stuff, and they don't fit the bed, so everyone tries to get enough material with their private spends to make their own cover and curtains. That's a privilege for LTIs [long-term inmates], but short termers get LTI privileges too, so they can make them. I didn't, I had the attitude that it didn't matter what you did to it, it was still a cell. You had a plastic white jug for washing water, a see-through plastic jug for your drinking water and a translucent plastic potty with a lid, and you had a hard-backed upstanding chair. Top-security men were allowed a soft armchair when they had the wing, but not the women. I wasn't even allowed a sketchbook when I first went there, or paints, and yet the men could have all sorts of things – paints, budgies, cooking facilities. Double standards again.

You had a special board for pinning things on, about 14″ by 16″ – tiny. You could only put things on there, not on the walls. You might be hiding a hole in the wall. You're not even allowed to put your furniture on the outside wall: your bed had to be at least six inches away from the wall, and my head used to get caught between the bars on the bed. Nothing must be near that wall in case you're digging your way out (and don't forget you're breaking out into a prison). You're not allowed pencil sharpeners, scissors or tweezers, a nail file or sponges. I don't know why we couldn't have sponges. The Salvation Army gave us all sponges one Christmas and some bath cubes and a bar of soap, and two days after Christmas: 'Please hand in your sponges, they're not allowed.' We had to march into the office and put our names down: 'Handed in', 'Handed in', 'Handed in.' They're all potty. Poor Sally Army had gone to all that trouble of buying us all these sponges. They give it out with one hand and take it back with the other.

Of course you had to keep your cell scrubbed out. You would do that whilst they did the bell, bar and bolts routine. What they do is they would come and check the bars in case you sawed through them, get up and stand all over your bed and pull at the bars, then check your emergency bell – it's not really a bell, but a little flap: remember the old-fashioned cars with the indicators? Like that. You press the bell and the flap pops up. Oh, you've got to laugh! Then they'd check the bolts. The doors are electronic with dirty great bolts top and bottom, but they still check the bolts in case they'd been nicked. Whilst they were doing this they'd look round your cell, look under your bed for bits of fluff, and they had this little book in which they'd write: No. 5 cell, 'DIRTY'! One bit of fluff, 'FILTHY'! A match, 'DISGUSTING. Hasn't been cleaned for years'!

You're expected to know their routine. Nobody tells you. You do learn off other inmates: I mean, if you don't ask, you don't get told, and I asked. Otherwise you're meant to be a mind reader. Another thing, because of the acoustics there, they shout your name. Geordies are hard to understand at the best of times, but in a place like that when they shout your name, they might be on the landings or on the flat part, and you might be in the middle, so by the time they've shouted it's bounced off all the walls and ceilings and comes out gaga. So you don't know you're being shouted at. It takes time for your ears to atune.

Next day the Chief Officer will see you. That wing was hers – her women, her wing, her way, her everything, and she ruled that wing. Even the governor or AG had no say. I mean, she was the matriarch. When I saw her she said, 'What are you doing in my prison?' I said, 'I didn't ask to come here.' 'Well, what are you doing here? You've only got three and a half years. These women of mine, do you understand, they're doing . . .' 'I don't know, you tell me.' 'Well, I can see you're a stroppy one.' There were women aged between eighteen and seventy when I was there, doing life. When you go to a place like that, you think how lucky you are to have such a small sentence. You can see a light at the end of the tunnel and you can be a bit buoyant, but when you see some of them who don't know when they're going to get out, it's horrible, awful. There were seventeen women from foreign countries when I was there – more than half. Virtually no concessions were made for them or their needs. Many can't speak the language. English is bad enough for some foreigners, but when it's Geordie dialect it's even worse. You start to get annoyed for them and you think, 'What the heck are they doing to these people?'

Your letters have to be in English. If they aren't, then you can't have them until they've been translated. That can some-times take weeks. I received a postcard from a friend in Holland. She said, 'Hello, how are you!', you know, and put her address. I was called over by one of the officers. She showed me the card and said, 'What's this?' and I said, 'It looks like a card for me.' 'What's this?' 'Oh, it's from my friend.' 'Next time you get one of these it will be sent to the censor's.' I said, 'But she's written in English.' 'This bit isn't.' 'That's her address.' 'It'll be sent to the censor's next time.' This was a senior officer telling me that a Dutch address should be written in English!

A typical day in Durham. They bang on your door at seven, just to see if you're alive. They told me that. You must move at seven, even if it's just to wave an arm in the air: if you're alive, just wave; don't bother if you're not. They may come round at 7.30 to see if you're out of bed. If not they start kicking the door. Usually I was still in bed, I couldn't see any reason to get up: what's the point? They don't open the door till eight, so you're just sitting there, may as well lay in bed. The facilities for washing are very slim, so you're hoping your door will be one of the first to be opened so you can get to a sink and at least clean your teeth. Everything is done in a great rush, because breakfast is brought over round 8.15.

You've got to get washed, go to toilet and slop out. Don't forget there's thirty-six women doing it and there's only six loos and twelve sinks. At 8.20 they start screaming, 'Get down for breakfast.' So you all have to get down and they tick you off on their little board. Then you go for breakfast in whatever time you've got left to throw it down your throat. At 8.25, they're shouting, 'Line up for work.'

There's no varied work. It's just working in the workroom and wing-cleaning. They like to keep you scrubbing on your knees for your first two months. I was made to scrub the whole of the workroom floor every day when I first went there, even though I've got a pin in my knee, which they didn't want to know about because you can kneel with one knee: you don't *need* both. If you're not on wing-cleaning or washing up the breakfast things, which everyone takes turns in, you're marched through to the workroom, where you're making NATO hats, NATO overalls, army belts and army hats. They even had American caps for the American bases, you know the blue peak ones? You're on piece work. You had to churn out approximately twenty-seven to thirty a day, which is heavy going – the hats come in about twelve sections – and you're given two weeks' training by another inmate. I don't know how many overalls you have to make, but one girl doesn't do the complete thing: she might do the bottom part and someone else does another part. Belts – you're talking about 800 a day to get your money. Bags – you have to do between 300 and 400 of them a day to get your money, which worked out at £3 a week when I was there. They stop 3p of it for newspapers. (Incidentally, you don't have a choice which ones they buy. They get the *Sun*, *Daily Mirror*, a local paper, and I think it was the *Mail* or the *Express*. You never saw *The Times* or the *Guardian* or anything like that. I did ask, but I didn't get anywhere.)

I was against anything nuclear on principle. They don't recognise principles: your work's your work and you should be grateful you *are* working. That's their attitude. Work is a privilege. So you're forced into working to make your life a little easier – so you can buy coffee if you don't like tea, a few little things like that. [Tea is the main drink in prison, always served with the milk already added. If the women wanted to drink coffee occasionally they had to buy it from their wages.] You're working against your principles, but the only thing you can do is blank it out.

The workroom's got no see-out windows. The windows have got those heavy panes in them, thick opaque bulletproof stuff, and the only air you get's from an extractor fan. There are skylight windows, but they always seemed to be stuck. The radio is on a tannoy system and it's always on Radio Two: can you imagine being forced to listen to Jimmy Young every day? There's a little annexe with short swing doors with glass in them where the toilets are. The toilets also have swing doors and they face the workshop, so you can see someone's head and legs whilst they're sitting on the toilet. If you want to go to the toilet you have to put your name on a list. There's three loos, but only one woman can go at a time: nobody must go if there's someone else in there. Even if you're dying to go or you've got diarrhoea – too bad! You put your hand up and wait till they call out your name. One day I was in there and this girl came running in: 'Oh, you're in here, Ginger, but I've got to go too.' I said, 'Suit yourself.' It was her neck not mine. But the next minute, because I was in the first loo, I got this officer leaning over the door. 'What are you doing in here?' I said, 'I got permission, I'm written down. Do you mind not leaning over the door when I'm going to the loo?' She was going on about my being in the loo with another person – 'It's against the rules' and so on. 'Well, she's not sitting in me lap' I said. I mean, really!

Anyway, after you've finished at the workroom, you get marched back to the wing, then exercise. If you don't get exercise – and you often don't – you're locked in. Dinner is around 11.30. The food generally was awful. It was all cooked in the men's prison and then carried over and left outside the gate, right next to the drain, so it was usually cold when we got it, no covers or anything. It used to worry us what the men had done to it, spat in it or something, especially if there had been stuff in the papers about any of us. If you don't want to eat for whatever reason, you're locked in. You can't sit with the others whilst they eat theirs. It's like you're being punished.

Then it's back to the workshop at 2.30 and 4.40 it's back to the wing. That's Monday to Friday. Saturday and Sunday you're allocated a job on the wing which you do for two months, then they change you round. It can be cleaning out the visiting room, scrubbing the showers or scrubbing the landings, even though they've all been done during the week. Cleaning is their main hobby! You're expected to scrub on your hands and knees in your own clothes, and don't forget you've only got three sets. You use one of those green pot scourers and a big bar of soap. When you've done your job you call the officer and say, 'I've finished, Miss, can you inspect my job?' and she inspects it and if it's not up to her standard you go back and do it again. I've gone back and cleaned a landing three times. If they've got a bee in their bonnet about you they'll make you do it again and again: you can see it, their power over you, the sort of gleam in their eye.

You're not allowed to do education in 'their' time. [Work time when the women are either machining in the workroom or cleaning.] The only people that can (and that's only in the mornings from 9.30 to 11.30) are women who can't read or write English. Any other education is very limited: you have to do it in your own time, including Open University. Say, for example, you book for maths, and maths is twice a week in the evening, and then you decide after going a few times that you don't want to go to maths classes after all. You *have* to stick it out until the term ends. If you don't want to go or you've got a headache, you're locked in. You've got to stick to your choice. They keep checking the classes, too. All classroom doors have a glass window, and if the officers look through and don't think you're working, they come in and tell you off. You might be discussing something, but their idea is that if you're doing Maths you've got to be writing figures all the time. That's why they hated the debating class: there we weren't writing with our heads down, and sometimes the air got a little high. They used to come in and stand there, waiting to see what was going to happen. They always have an over-the-top attitude.

At the weekends you could have visits which start at 1.30. Tea's around three o'clock at weekends, four during the week. On Saturday and Sunday they'll sometimes show a video, which we've paid for out of our wing fines: the money gets stopped from your wages, and it goes into a wing fund. But we don't have a choice about what we see. The men [male prisoners in the men's section of Durham Prison] choose. So we got pornographic films! The men have them in the morning, we have them in the afternoon, films like the 'Porky' films, or really nasty stuff, 'Chain Saw Massacre', the Manson killings – really horrible ones, cut 'em up, you know? Killings, horror or sex. Sometimes there was the odd comedy, but they always revolved around sex.

Sunday, a male screw brings over an 8½ mm film and projector. I remember one Easter he showed the Oliver Reed film where he was a Roman Catholic priest and it was about his exploits with the nuns – you know, confessions and whippings. I thought it was a bit ironic to have that at Easter. There was a lot of Catholics on the wing and all. After that we had our supper – a cup of tea and a stale bun, the yellow peril [traditional prison cake containing a particularly lurid yellow food colouring]. Between 7.30 and eight you have to get your drinking water and your washing water into your cell. You needed washing water in case you had to use your pot, or for washing out clothes or for washing in the morning if you couldn't face fighting over the sinks. The doors are locked electronically at 8.30. The lights are controlled from outside. They come round at ten, eleven and twelve, and if they'd forgotten to switch off your light, you were lumbered with it all night. imany's the time that happened to me. There's one night officer you never ever saw because she was never on day duty. She knows you but you don't know her. She's just an eye in the spy-hole and a disembodied voice. They come round quite often to inspect you during the night. There was always clattering: clatter, bang, up and down the stairs. They were open-plan metal stairs and they echo all the way through.

Any time, day or night, you're never without noise in prison.

So that's the routine, Christmas Day as well, every day of the year. It never ever changes.

Because it's Category A, you get a lot of searching in Durham. You're searched before and after the workroom, before and after a visit, and that will often be a complete strip search. Every week to ten days, you get a complete cell and body search. No reason: they just do it, it keeps the staff busy. They come for you in the workroom and you lose pay because you're doing piece-work. We used to dread it. You march off with the officers, get taken up to the cell, and they tell you to strip off, sometimes down to your underwear, sometimes everything. You hand your clothes to the officer. She searches through them and hands them back, and you put them back on. They start searching through your cell. They rake everything out of your wardrobe, they pull out your papers, everything, and you've got to put it back. They pull your cabinet out, the wardrobe out, and look underneath and on top; they take all your books off, and check the number of books you've got against the amount you're allowed; they strip your bed, they take the rubber off the bottom of the bed legs, take the mattress cover off – and they are hell to get back on, especially if you've got a tight one. Oh, my God! They take your pillowcase off your pillow. They search *every-thing*. They stand on your bed and look out of your window, in case you've got a horse and cart out there, three floors up. But they won't let you put the stuff back then – oh no! You've got to do it in your own time. They take you back to the workroom or whatever and during the dinner hour you've got to do the bloody room because if you don't, you get put on report for having an untidy room. Oh, they wreck rooms. I've seen girls in tears over their rooms, they wreck 'em.

Anyway, that's what you call a normal cell search. Then comes what they call a complete wing search, usually in your time, a Saturday. You're locked in and they bring the men over with the dogs. They search everything – toilets, showers, landings, everything. You hear them running up and down stairs, and you hear the dogs barking. Then they go to the cells, one after the other, and they take everything out but the bed: they can't get that through the doors without dismantling it and only the inmates know how to do that. Everything in your cell's pulled out on the landing, and the whole thing takes a day. You have to eat all your meals in the cell and you lose an entire day.

If the staff get bored and all the girls are getting on, they don't like it, so they start going round stirring up trouble: divide and rule. Some of them do like trouble because it makes the time go quicker and they're so fond of telling us that they are doing a sentence as well. It's a well-known fact. They'll go into a prisoner's room, say something and leave that prisoner with that thought and then it'll start trouble.

The wing is bound to affect the officers. It's so depressing. Can you imagine, a nice summer's day and they've got to walk into that tomb where nothing penetrates. It must affect them as well. They're bound to stagnate and become bitter, and who do they take it out on? Some of them get jealous of things we have. If we're sent letters they'll say things like, 'Who would want to write to you monsters?' That's how people see women on H wing: monsters. 'Why should anybody care about you?' If you've had a parcel, say it's clothing, they'll say, 'You can't have this clothing. Oh, look at this, look at the label on this' – you know, anything. If it's something they can pick on, you suffer for it. You do get some of them that come in saying, 'I care.' Fair enough, they might start off with that attitude, wanting to help. But if they're going to get on with their colleagues and they're going to be seen to be doing the job correctly, they can't carry on, they just can't do it. If they cared about the prisoners they'd be told they were fraternising too much. We had an officer who was ostracised by her colleagues: 'Going in a pantomime with criminals?' We used to call her Nellie, and they didn't like that either because she didn't say anything, she'd laugh, and they didn't like it because she was getting too friendly with 'them'. The pressures from her colleagues was such that she had to change. She got harder.

All most officers want to hear is gossip on another inmate. If you talk about your own problem, whatever it is, outside, inside, they shrug because it's boring; only if it's about another inmate will they listen. They don't want to hear about problems because they can't help you. They'd lose their job if they did.

Those of us who are 'the disturbances' are watched extra carefully and often put on report. The officers may turn a blind eye to the women that are friendly to them, say if they have something in their cell not legal by the guidelines. So if you're not friendly with the screw, she's not going to turn a blind eye, she's going to put you on report. It's working against the grain all the time.

There's a punishment cell in Durham, not a punishment block. It's on the flat, off what's called the blue room, which is a little courtyard with drains and things like that. The floor is like outside paving – this is where we had gym. In the winter it's very damp, cold and wet, so there's no fresh air in the punishment cell. It's a strip cell, with only one mattress on the floor. Because it's on the flat, it's tucked right away under the stair part so you can't get messages through. You can't even get to know if a person's still alive or ill. If you cut up or do anything which they think is a disturbance they'll put you down there. I was put there on my last night in Durham; they thought it fitting that I should taste what it's like. They'd never got me down there in all the time I'd been there, and they said it was for my own good because I was upset. So I left Durham from there. What a goodbye!

Usually for punishment, you get locked in your own cell. Now you also get locked on what they call the hospital wing, but it's not really a hospital – it's for punishment. There's four cells there. If you get put behind the door [slang for cellular confinement, a punishment meted out when a prisoner breaks the rules], you can spend it up there. The cells have got small windows and they're right at the end of the block within a caged area. H Wing is bad enough, but when you're behind the door and you're a smoker it's torture. Other prisons, if you're behind the door, they allow you a cigarette after each meal. On H wing that's not allowed, so if you're stuck behind the door for seven or fourteen days you can go mad. You're not allowed your canteen, you're not allowed private spends.

The feeling runs through the majority of women in Durham that you've got to be on the good side of the staff because they hold the key to your release or your getting out of Durham. You know at the end of their shift the officers have got to write a report about you. If you're doing life or you're in a long time, your main goal is getting out of Durham, and the only way is to be very good and do 'Yes Miss, no Miss and three bags full miss', go to the workshop and turn out 31,000 whatever a week. Don't question anything, do everything right, and that way you'll get out of Durham. That's your only goal.

Visits were difficult. Nothing is private in that place – nothing, nothing. I was told to stop whispering on one of my visits: my visitor had come 700 miles and could only stay half an hour because I was on report, so she was punished as well. I wasn't allowed to give her a cup of tea. I was told to speak up and so was she. Sometimes there were more screws in the visiting room than visitors. You can't say anything personal without them hearing, and you know they'll discuss with each other what you've said. It's impossible to keep relationships going; many friends and families give up visiting. I stopped my girlfriend from coming. You've got to think before you say anything, you can't be yourself, and they can't be themselves – it's a strain. You can cut the atmosphere with a knife, that feeling of intensity, that everything you say is being listened to, and if you touch, or you hold hands, you get told off. You greet your visitor when they come in, but after that the table is between you, and you just sit there, looking at each other. It causes this tension which builds up, and my visitor would go away and she'd write things like, 'I'm sorry the visit was so bad. We talked but I didn't speak.'

There was no sports facilities except the blue room, which is a laugh. It's just an area of the prison which is cut off, and you were nervous to play volleyball because you daren't tackle – it was concrete and all bumpy, and there was the drains there and if the ball bounced on that it just died on you. It was always so cold and damp and there was no toilets and showers, so people avoided going. They got hardly any exercise, except walking around the yard, and people didn't want to do that either. Most of the women were unfit. With my colitis I have to have a certain amount of exercise and when I don't do it I get worse. Of course the diet didn't help. But it's amazing how the human mind can fight things. I didn't want 'rest in cell'. It's like a punishment: they might as well put RIP instead of RIC on your door. And with colitis if you've got to use a potty, it's bad, it's horrible. So you avoid that, you fight it, you fight your illness. When you get out of Durham and get sent to another place, you collapse with it. It's like holding your breath and then suddenly breathing again so that when you do, you go down. I spent the last few weeks of my sentence in Askham Grange prison hospital. You relax and that's it, you go down. That's when I was told I was Labour II as well. [Women are classified for work: Labour I – any work; Labour II – not heavy work; Labour III – only light work.] In Durham they didn't recognise illness. Women had heart troubles; another had fluid on the lung; there were skin problems, because of insufficient daylight. Five women had hysterectomies whilst I was there, and nearly all the women had problems with periods, and of course psychological problems. Everyone has a mental problem: schizophrenia, paranoia and phobias – claustrophobia, agoraphobia. They just don't want to know. They just say, 'We don't know about it, we haven't said you're disabled so you're not.' So that's difficult to cope with. If you've got a phobia, it's used against you. I asked for months and months to see a psychiatrist, because it's up to the nursing staff to put you down. The senior nurse would say, 'Oh what do you want to see the psychiatrist for?' and the chances are you wouldn't get to see one.

I was in the army, I learnt Queens Regulations. I was a military policewoman. When I went to other units they knew I was a threat to them, because if they did anything to anybody, that girl would say to me, 'I'm being put on charge so and so', and I'd say, 'But you can argue this and that.' I became known as a barrack-room lawyer. It's the same in prison. You need to get hold of the rules and regulations, which I asked for at each of the prisons I went to. Even the fact of asking is a bad mark against you. They don't want you to know the rules and regulations because they break them so often. A lot of prison staff are ex-army, and being ex-army myself I understood the slang and everything. I was a thorn in their sides, a very big thorn. They kept insisting I'd been in prison before, because I had this ability: I knew how they worked.

I've been in institutions all my life. I started off in boarding schools, then the navy and the army. Institutional life for me is not new. If you want things improving for yourself, and for others as well, don't accept things. People say that you can't change the system. If that was true we'd still be in Newgate on straw. So it does change. But it's got to be changed by the people they accuse of kicking the system.

Since her release, Ginger has been living in London. Although she left H wing two years ago, it has a continuing effect on her life, and she has great difficulty in sleeping. She attends art classes at CAST, an organisation for women ex-prisoners, and is actively involved in the campaign to close H wing.

Mary

*Mary is Scottish, and at nineteen was the youngest woman we spoke
to. She was staying at a hostel for ex-prisoners in London. She had
been released from a Youth Custody sentence three months before
and, like everyone released from Youth Custody, was on licence.
This entails regular appointments with a probation officer.*

I was born in Glasgow in 1967 and I stayed with my mum and
dad, and then they got divorced when I was young and that
broke us all up. It gutted me 'cause I loved my dad. But he still
used to beat my mum up after the divorce, so I won't speak to
him now. Then she got married to my stepdad, and I love him
more than my real dad. We moved to Fort William when I was
about nine. I was missing Glasgow, so I stole my mum's family
allowance book and ran away back there. She got me charged
with theft so I got put in a children's home. I was nine years old
and I've been in institutions, assessment centres and List D
schools ever since. [A List D school is the Scottish equivalent of
an approved school.]

I don't see my mum now. I can't go and see her because I do
fraud. My mum, stepdad, all my family's got chequebooks,
even my little brother Steven. She doesn't trust me not to take
them; she doesn't trust me at all. I wouldn't steal off them, but
she says I've done it in the past, so I'd do it again.

I was the youngest in the children's home. The others was
fourteen and fifteen. They were all into glue and the drugs. One

day there were about five of us together and they said, 'Take some glue, take some glue.' I said, 'No, I don't want it', so I got called a coward. So in the end, I started on the glue and I was on it for about four and a half years. Then they started me on the dope. I wouldn't touch heroin: no way, it's a fool's game.

Whenever the home thought I was getting too heavily involved with certain people, they'd move me. I was in one home in Ballahulish, just outside Fort William, and they moved me up to Inverness, but I got worse into the glue because I was the youngest again. I was only about thirteen at the time. I asked my mum if I could come home and she said 'no'. I said, 'Fair enough, don't bother speaking to me then', and we didn't speak much from when I was thirteen until I was about seventeen.

One day I looked in the mirror and I thought, 'You'll end up killing yourself.' So I just stopped. When you glue-sniff you get spots on your face and all my spots went away. I really looked a lot healthier. It took a lot to stop doing it, but I did. I don't speak to my friends who still use it. I won't have anything to do with drugs at all now.

I was in children's homes and List D schools until I was sixteen. I was there for stupid things like theft, just to get me some money, 'cause all the people I went round with were older than me. I find people my age very boring. I loved my List D school. If someone told me, 'You've got to do three years in a List D school or twelve months in a prison', I'd go to a List D school as long as it was the same one I was at. All my mates were there – mates from Fort William and from Glasgow. It was just a good laugh. We weren't allowed to stand near the windows because that attracted the boys, so that was bad, but we didn't have any locked doors, nothing like that. Me and my big sister was in it together. My sister was in trouble as well, though she's never been in prison. I'm the only bad one, or so my mum tells me.

When I was fourteen I met this bloke called Tam. He taught me how to forge signatures, so I started doing chequebooks. He was thirty-four. I was going out with him for getting on three years, but we broke up and I got married to someone else. My husband was twenty-four and I was sixteen. I only lived with my husband for a few weeks, then I left him because he beat me up all the time. As my mum says, at least I won't grow old and say I didn't get married. I was just a silly little girl then – you know, every little girl's dream is getting married – I thought, 'Oh, marriage – brilliant', so I did it. Never again. I made my mistakes young. My mum liked him before we got married, but after we got married and he was beating me up, she went right off him, because my dad used to beat her up. She knew what I was going through.

My mother-in-law took me stealing with her. She used to steal as well. She got me to do chequebooks because she wanted money for a new carpet, and then my husband grassed me up, and that's what I got the jail for. Three months. I got him beat up for grassing – he's never grassed on anyone since. I haven't spoken to him or phoned him for two years now. I know if I speak to him I've got less chance of getting a divorce because they'll say I've communicated with him and I don't want that. I want the divorce as soon as possible.

I was sent to Cornton Vale prison. It was a nice prison, apart from the uniforms we had to wear: a big flarey skirt, the jumpers were well-ripped and everything, and we had an old parka jacket, and the shoes, they were like traffic warden's shoes. It was horrible, I wouldn't have dressed my granny like it. Cornton Vale didn't look like the prisons you get down here. It's really modern and had just a fence round it: it looked just like little Barratt houses. The food was a lot better than down here, too, because there was six or seven different houses and only five or six girls to a house, so we cooked our own meals and obviously did decent ones. The food was always hot, it was very nice. But I was scared at first. I thought, 'Och, it'll just be like my List D school', but it wasn't. It was a lot tougher. You had to be in bed by a certain time, or you got put on report. I wouldn't do my time there again. I did just over two months because I lost some remission. I was the youngest in the unit again – I've always been the youngest, except on my last sentence.

I went back with Tam after my first sentence and everything

was okay for about six or seven months. We had a wee flat a couple of miles outside Inverness. Of course, I was doing the chequebooks and so was he, so our wee home was like a palace – beautiful. One day I went to British Home Stores at Clydebank to get a suit because my grandad had just died, so I thought I'd better have something decent to wear. I went and got a beautiful suit, but I must have made a mistake on one of the cheques and they found me out. They went, 'Hang on till we check this up', and the police came in and lifted me. I was remanded for about three days and then they put me straight back to Cornton Vale. I thought they might have given me a day's parole to go to the funeral but they didn't. I got nine months for that.

Cornton Vale was exactly the same. All the screws still remembered me. They said, 'What are you doing back here?' The screws were nice, they were really good. I was working making mail bags and chef's trousers for the boys' prison, and the dust coats that the male officers wear, like when they're out on the farms. Boring, but it passed the day, I suppose, better than getting locked up. I was getting £4.50 to £5 a week. Down here I was only getting £1.35 a week, but here you can get money sent in to you to buy toiletries and things; up there the only time you could get money sent in was for your birthday, your Christmas and your New Year.

After that sentence I thought I'd keep out of trouble, so I moved down here to London with Tam. I thought, 'I'll make a new start, I don't know nobody except for Tam, so it'll be okay.' I intended to stay out of trouble and then, because he was signing on for the two of us and we weren't getting that much money, I couldn't handle being skint. I'd never been without money, I've always done the books, so I went out and done them again. I was doing really well on them, I never got caught. But one day my luck changed. There used to be a pub called the Phoenix in Euston Station, and I was in there drinking with my best friend. I *thought* she was my best friend. We'd had an argument and she went up to the bar and told the barman what age I was, because I was only sixteen at the time. I thought she was going up to get another drink, because she brought the drinks back, but five minutes later the police came in and lifted me. All they charged me for was under-age drinking. Then I got moved from station to station. I was in Paddington first, then they searched me and found a chequebook, credit cards, driver's licence and what have you, so they moved me to Holborn police station, then Albany police station and then to Goodge Street police station, and then back to Albany. It took about a week and a half for them to take me up to court, which was really disgusting, because I had a white jumper and a white skirt on at the time, and they wouldn't let me have a wash or a bath. You can imagine what colour I was going into court. Tam didn't get done because I wouldn't grass him up. He'd done time before he met me, about eighteen years altogether, with all his sentences. I always knew I would end up in prison for chequebooks. I knew I couldn't get away with it for ever and they'd catch up with me sometime – they were bound to. I just took it day by day. If I got caught, I got caught. Tam knew I'd never grass him because one thing I'm not is a grass.

When I went into Holloway, I had black eyes and my lip was out here. I got beat up by the police, because I wouldn't tell them who Tam was and where he stayed and all the rest of it. I was in Holloway for three months waiting for my trial. When I went to court I got given twelve months. I got twelve months for every cheque that I wrote out and twelve months for deception, twelve for dishonestly handling and twelve for theft. But he ran them all concurrent which was lucky, because I got thirty-four lots of twelve months. He paused a wee moment before he said concurrent, and I was well shocked.

I didn't like it one bit in Holloway. I didn't like it at all. We were banged up all the time except for exercise and coming out for meals. Sometimes we had to have our meals in our rooms. We were banged up straight after tea till until about 7.30 or eight the next morning, which was rubbish. At Cornton Vale, you were allowed out all the time, we had association every night. In Cornton Vale, you go into reception, you see the nurse right away, you get dressed and you go straight to your unit. I was sitting in reception at Holloway for about an hour and a half before they saw me. And then they gave me this horrible food.

I was drinking heavy before I went in. I used to drink an awful lot, so the doctor put me on to Atavan [a tranquilliser], just to calm me down. One night the nurse wouldn't give me it, so I freaked. I waited till the next morning till we got out of our cells, and I just grabbed her. I don't know why, probably because I hadn't had any Atavan all day – I was on it four times a day. So I just grabbed her and started punching her. I got her head in between a door and slammed it. I lost three weeks' remission for that and she was off for about a week and a half with concussion. But, as the doctor said, she had no right to refuse me my medication. If I'd been written up for it, I should've got it. All the way through my sentence, until just before I got out, I was on valium and other medicine at nights. I didn't want to need it out there as well. I've done really well without it this time.

I spent a few months in Holloway and then they moved me to Bullwood Hall. That's where they send all the bad girls. I remember when I first went there, I went into the courtyard in a van. It was like a concentration camp – big high walls and barbed wire on top of the wall. I thought, 'Where the hell am I? Have they taken me to the right place?' It looked terrible. The units were nice. I was only on a small unit because they said I was unstable, that I couldn't get put on a big unit because it would crack me up. They moved me around at first. Sometimes I was in a single cell, other times I had to share. They put me in with this girl Karen and we got on really well, and then she went home and they put me into a single again. Then I was put in with another girl, Ann, to see if I could calm her down. I was in with Ann until I came out.

At one time they put Ann down the block for cutting her arms up and so I thought, 'She's not going down alone. If she goes down, I go down.' Simple as that. So, one night, they wouldn't let me have a jug of water at bed-time, so I cracked up. I still had a wee bit of water in my jug and I went, 'You will'na let me have a jug of water, take this then' – and I threw it on them.

Twenty-eight days down the block. I was well sick. Ann got out of the block before I did. I got a letter from her the other week: she's on punishment again. She's missing me and she's cut herself up and she tried to hang herself. I feel really sorry for her. She is doing six years for criminal damage, and she's only about nineteen.

There wasn't much bullying. There was a crowd of us who all used to stick together, and if a screw was getting onto one of us the others would say, 'You're bang out of order.' There was a time when stupid things like someone's tobacco was going missing, someone else's talc, someone's soap, so we had a house meeting and we found out who it was – this little feeble girl – and we said, 'Right, in future you'll not be trusted, you'll be watched all the time.' Well, after about three months she stopped it, so we could all trust her again. It was better to get her in a group and give her a lecture on it instead of just one-to-one, because she'll feel more sorry if everybody's getting onto her. The girls organised that. The screws wouldn't join in a meeting unless we put in an application to the governor to ask if we could have a proper house meeting with screws and the girls. We just had meetings because we wanted to. I don't know if other houses had them. I didn't really mix with the other houses.

It was a nice prison though. I think if I had to go back inside that would be the prison I'd want to go to again – Bullwood Hall. I made the best of my time – I got a certificate in community care. I just applied to go to the Education Department and do a course, and they put me onto a community care course which lasted three months. We got three days out – the first one we went to a playgroup and the second one we went into an elderly people's home and then we went to a handicapped centre. It was really good. We had a really good laugh, like if someone on the course had a problem we'd all just sit down and discuss the problem and then it would be okay again. Like if one of the girls was getting onto one of the screws but the screw hadn't done anything, someone would go up to her and say, 'Listen, you're out of order.' At the end of it, I sat an exam which I passed. I'm starting college in September to do community care, because I've really decided this time I'm staying out. Definitely.

The food in Bullwood Hall was disgusting. I'm not allowed to eat anything with fat because of my stomach ulcers, and I used to get poached eggs and boiled potatoes all the time. It used to crack me up. I saw the governor and said, 'When I leave here I'm going to *look* like a poached egg or boiled potato.' So, after that, instead of getting fried fish and fried chips, I used to get my fish and chips baked, which was far nicer anyway. I started to enjoy the food after that. Everyone there was putting on weight and I was losing it – I lost three and a half stone in nine months. Some of the screws at Bullwood were okay. They were really good to you if you had a problem; they'd sit down and listen to you. But some of them were key-happy bastards: 'In your cell', 'Lock up.' At weekends if we had no association we were banged up from four in the afternoon until eight the next morning. I don't like getting locked up – I feel like an animal.

I was shocked by the screws when I came down here to Holloway. They didn't really care what happened; it's just a case of lock-up, lock-up. It's just wrong. Like I had this friend and one night she couldn't breathe properly. She had asthma and it took about three-quarters of an hour before a screw would unlock the door to let her out and take her to the hospital wing. It was really annoying because her breathing was really, really bad. There was four of us in the cell and we were all really worried about her. It was disgusting – I don't agree with that at all.

The first time I went to prison I told my mum it was for theft. I said I was out shoplifting. And this time, when I got my sentence, she didn't even know I was in London. I thought I'd not tell them till I saw whether I'd get a sentence, 'cause I might have got off with it. So after three and a half months, when I got sentenced, the probation let me phone her up from Holloway. She said, 'Where are you staying now?' and I said, 'London.' She said, 'Well, what's your address and I'll write to you.' I said, 'Have you got a pen handy, ma?' She said, 'Yes.' I went, 'HMP

Holloway.' She said, 'What? My wee baby's in prison?' I was always the pet of the family and she started crying and she asked, 'How long did you get?' and I went, 'Twelve months', and she went, 'Oh, my wee baby got twelve months.' It made me feel really guilty. I couldn't do it to her again. It really hurt her the last time. It hurt my dad, and even my sisters and brothers were all crying when she told them I was in prison again. They weren't so worried when I was in Cornton Vale; this was my first time out of Scotland, so they were more worried. While I was on remand, my sister booked in at a hotel down here and she was up seeing me every day. But after that she says, 'Sorry, I can't come up and see you again because it's going to cost too much.' I said, 'I understand that. I appreciate you coming to see me all the way from Scotland.' It was nice of her. She didn't have to do it.

I only saw the welfare a couple of times in prison. I used to write to my mum near enough every day and I kept asking her how my Uncle Bobby was, because he had a stroke and gangrene in one of his toes and he was diabetic so he had to get his leg took off at the knee. I got the probation to find out how he was, and they told me he had died a few days before. They wouldn't give me parole to go to his funeral. I was a wreck, because me and my uncle Bobby were really close – I used to go up and see him at the hospital every day and bring him up his diabetic chocolate. It cut me up at the time. I cracked up with my mum because she hadn't told me. She wrote back and said she didn't want that I should worry while I was in prison, so I wrote back and said, 'At least it would have been better coming from you than the probation service', which it would have.

I deserved my last sentence. I knew it was coming. I don't think anything else would have worked because at that time I was still knocking about with Tam. I would have ended up doing my books again. Tam wrote me a letter while I was in prison saying he couldn't handle me being inside, so he went back with his wife. So I wrote back saying, 'That's all right. Fuck off you no-good cunt' and all the rest of it. At first Tam was writing to me every day, so I got letters off him, and I got a couple off my mum – one of them was a birthday card, and one a Christmas card and that was that. My big sisters and my little brothers used to write to me all the time, and my granny, and all my aunties and uncles. NACRO arranged a prison visitor to come and see me every two weeks, she was really nice. I still keep in touch with her.

I've had just about every sentence a court can give out. In Scotland you can't go to prison until you're sixteen, so a List D school or an assessment centre was the only two places you could go to, which is good. I think it's ridiculous that down here you can put someone that's under sixteen in prison. I've had probation once and I got two fines and four 'Admonished'. I got off with quite a bit – the judge did give me a couple of good chances. Then I got probation, then they got that fed up they just sent me down. Can't blame them, right enough. My Youth Custody licence and probation finishes next month, and I'll be glad when that's finished, but at least there's a probation officer you can turn to if you're in trouble. I think after I come off probation I might go on voluntary probation 'cause I'm used to it. I've almost always been on supervision since I was in children's homes. I'd be lost without it. I wouldn't know where to go for anything. They are helpful – well, my one is anyway.

I always went to church in there – I still do. I've gone to church since I was small. And Confession on a Saturday. I used to tell the priest I'd done this and I'd done that and I'd feel a lot better for telling him. He didn't used to say anything. They're not allowed to tell the police. He used to give me my penance and ask me to stop doing it. I used to say, 'What? On the money I get?' Tam used to keep all the money and pay the bills and do the shopping because he knew I'd just go to the pub and drink it.

When I came out my two friends made up a blind date with this bloke I'm going out with now. We've been together ever since. It's really good. I've quietened down a lot now and I don't drink that often – about once every three weeks – 'cause my boyfriend doesn't really drink. Last night was the first time I've really been drunk since I got out – I was paralytic that night. I don't take any tranquillisers. I'm determined I'm not going to go back on them. When I was on them in prison I didn't know what I was doing. I was all mixed up: I'd be up one minute and down the next. They cracked me up. There was twenty-five of us on my house, and four or five of us were on tranquillisers. We didn't used to take them properly; we used to spit them into a cup and then if we felt really depressed we'd just take a lot. That used to knock me out for a couple of days. But I'd never attempt to kill myself. Life's too good to waste. I can see people's reasons for cutting up and things like that if they were doing life or really, really long sentences. But people like me doing a stupid twelve months – there's no need for it at all. These scars were done five years ago and I'm going to have them for the rest of my life. I regret it now. Me and my mate was glue-sniffing and she took a razor to my arm and I took a razor to hers. I don't know why people cut themselves – just boredom, because there's nothing to do. I want to get plastic surgery to get rid of everything now – my scars and my tattoos. I'm going to have a discussion with a plastic surgeon next week, because they stop me from going for jobs. I wanted to work in McDonalds 'cause they were looking for people, so I went in for an interview and they refused me because I had tattoos.

If people ask me if I've ever been in trouble I'm always honest. If they ask if it's worth it, I'll always say, 'No, it's not worth it at all' which it isn't. I mean, that was twelve months out of my life. I could have been doing anything in that twelve months. Quite a few of the friends I did my time with are still in there, so I should just count my blessings. I've been tempted since I've come out, but I wouldn't like to go back, definitely not. The worst thing was when you got banged up and you looked out of your window and it was still broad daylight – it really used to crack me up, to think I could be at the pub, or up the dance, or going to the pictures. It used to really depress me. The worst thing they can do is take away your freedom. Lock me up in the fucking Ritz and it would still be bad. I hate my freedom being took away from me. I like to be moving about all the time, and going places, even if it's only down to Trafalgar Square to see all the birdies – it's still somewhere to go. I got out three months ago. I'm only just getting adjusted to having hold of my own money and going out when I want, going to bed when I want and getting up when I want. If they put me inside again, it would really crack me up. It would be a lot harder: I don't know why, it just would. I would lose my chance of going to college. And I'm just getting my family trusting me again. If I go back inside I'd lose that, and I'd probably end up doing the same as the rest of them, cutting myself. Eventually my family will trust me, when they see I've kept out of trouble and everything. It'll take them about a year. I've got to make a go of it, make something of my life.

A lot of the people I met in prison shouldn't have been there. There was one girl, she was in there for being drunk and incapable and for breach of the peace, and she got four months – I thought that was barmy. There was another one, she was about eight and a half months pregnant, and she got twelve months for stealing a jumper from M & S. They shouldn't have given her a sentence like that. She kept the baby until it was four months old, and then she had to hand it out. I don't think you should be able to have kids in a prison anyway, because that way it's like your kids doing your sentence with you.

What changes should they make to prison? They shouldn't bang us up as often. I think that's very bad. They should have a better relationship with the screws and the inmates. It could be better, because you do get some screws that are willing to talk to you, but there's others that don't give a fuck. They just sit down and say, 'You've done bad to get in here', which we all know we have. When they put your problems aside like that, all the anger just bottles up. That's how I used to feel if someone wouldn't talk to me: my anger just boiled and boiled and boiled, and in the end I'd just crack. Every time I cracked, they just told me to go and see the shrink. I'd lose my temper and throw things about. Tables would go flying, chairs would go flying, anyone who was in my way would get a punch in the mouth. I used to be very bad, but now I've quietened down a lot. I'm getting older; I suppose I've grown up. And I don't want to waste my life in prison.

MARY

Soon after we saw Mary she left the hostel, and has not been heard of since. She did not start the community care course she had been hoping to do at the local college.

Lee

Lee was twenty-three when we spoke to her and was living with her girlfriend in a flat in South London. She was unemployed. She spent a little over two years in prison.

I was born in Norwich. My family was well known in the whole town for troublemakers – I've got four brothers and a little stepsister. My mother died when I was nine; my father, who's Jamaican, remarried about two years ago. We've just never got on, ever since I can remember. From the time I was four my mother had thrombosis, kept going in and out of hospital. Dad would never take any care of none of us. We all went to different foster parents when she went to hospital. I had to do everything Dad said. He was strict because I was supposed to grow up the perfect little daughter (which I haven't done), marry, have children and everything. My brothers had much more freedom than I did.

After my mum died I had to do the cooking and the cleaning and the washing. I suppose it was expected of me. It was the natural thing to come to me. I never really took to school. I took a lot of time off, and when I went to big school I was only there for six weeks before I got expelled for hitting a teacher. I was living with my auntie at this time. She said she'd have me because I kept running away from the foster and children's homes. She never knew I got expelled, because I was still getting up and going to school with the rest and coming home at the same time. I'd go down town or something. When she did find out, she and I had a big argument: she'd do anything for me, but I went too far. I was a handful, a difficult kid. But it was only when mum died that things got on top of me. I didn't care about anybody, I didn't care about getting into trouble, I didn't care about nothing. I couldn't really talk to my auntie because she had her own problems. I couldn't talk to my own brothers, I hardly saw them from year to year. My father, I wouldn't even dream of talking to him about anything, I was petrified of my father. So really there was no one I could turn to. I think I was one of them kids that didn't want to be loved.

I grew up with the attitude that no one was going to boss me around. I had the attitude that if I want to fight I'll fight, and if I want to get drunk I'll get drunk. It meant year after year getting into more and more trouble.

My auntie went down to Social Services because I was beyond control, and they put me in a children's home. I didn't get on there; I run away the same day. They came and got me back, but they couldn't keep me there. So they had case conferences and decided I would go to an approved school. I really had no say in the matter, I was twelve. The approved school was in London, in Eltham. It was great, it was, just like a big happy family, all girls. The only thing I didn't agree with was going to church every morning and church every evening and saying prayers before meals and all that. I just couldn't get into that. I'm not Catholic, that's what I don't understand: I'm Church of England, but they sent me to a Catholic school. But they were very good to me in that school. It was run by nuns, and they were all very nice. I loved it there. We used to do plays, like 'Pirates of Penzance', that was really good, and sports day and Scottish dancing and Irish dancing. I really enjoyed it. There was always lots to do. You had to go to school as well, but that was all in the grounds: they didn't push you. They'd say the work's got to be done, but sometimes I would do it, sometimes I wouldn't; sometimes I'd copy other people's. If you were good you could do evening classes – sewing, cooking and things like that.

I had to leave when I was sixteen as I was too old to stay there.

When I left, where did I go? Straight back to Norwich, and to foster parents. My dad didn't want me; I wouldn't have gone anyway. I couldn't go to my auntie, neither. She was ill and it wouldn't have been fair. I wouldn't impose on anybody. So I went to these foster parents, and they wouldn't let me go out in the evenings. I said, 'Can I go out?' and they said 'No.' I went to my probation officer and she told me to give it a week, and then another week. I had a friend in Norwich who I often used to go and see; I ended up staying at her place.

The Social Services couldn't find me. My friend was living on her own in a house with a couple of kids. We'd been to school together, same age and everything; she had twins when she was sixteen. She wasn't married and she'd really got herself together. I thought, 'This is the life, come and go as you like.'

I started to get into trouble. I did the dirty on her: I broke into her gas meter. And I was going out daily doing homes [burglaries]. I didn't sign on, I never really knew much about that. The truth is, I couldn't take the shame because I didn't know how to fill in a form or anything, so I didn't bother. I used to go out doing burglaries – jewellery and things – and sell the stuff off, virtually anything to get a bit of money in my pocket. Someone might say, 'Go and do that for me', and I'd go out and do it. Then I was doing too much and I got caught; someone grassed on me. I was sixteen and six months pregnant. I didn't want the baby. I tried to do everything, but it just wouldn't go. I suppose really down deep I couldn't do it, you know what I mean? Anyway, I got caught and got a borstal sentence. I'd been in trouble ever since the age of twelve, shoplifting and everything, I'd been in court before. I got fines and cautions; I'd been on probation thousands of times for stupid things. I suppose I'd been lucky, really; I was always in trouble. Altogether I had sixty-five charges, all of them for burglary or violence. I always said to my auntie and my friends that I'd go to prison, but when I did, I was shocked. I was really shocked. I thought, 'On my own and with the baby and that. I can't handle that.'

I went to Holloway first and then I went to Styal – that's the only prison that will have young pregnant women. I don't know, I think I'm a lucky person, because when I go to prison I seem to get on with everyone, and they get on with me. When they took me into Holloway I didn't know what to do, what to say or nothing. I was literally shaking. When I walked into the main room it was packed. This was at midnight – I don't know what the hell was going on, but that room was packed, I've never seen so many girls in it, all sitting there, for this crime and that. One girl spoke to me. She asked me my name, and I told her. She asked me what I was in for and she said, 'You're pregnant?' and I said, 'Yeah.' She said, 'You'll be all right then.' I said, 'What do you mean by that?' She told me I'd go to the mother and baby unit. 'You'll be all right.' I had a medical examination. They checked to see if the baby was okay; they checked my hair for lice; checked me below; then they took me straight onto the mother and baby wing. She was right.

They told me what I could have – visits and stuff; what clothes – three sets of clothes and skirts, shirts. Then they took me to my cell. I was on my own at first, which I didn't really mind, but during the early morning they came and put me in another cell with other people, six girls, fine girls. I went in, and everyone said, 'Hello, what's your name?' That was really nice. I was quite shocked, actually, I really was. Going from the first bit, when I just walked into prison and seeing all the girls – some heavy girls with different attitudes – then I was on the mother and baby unit and everyone being so nice . . . they made me feel at home. I knew it wasn't home, but they made me join in. They was lovely, they really was.

I was only there for about a week, and I was moved to Styal. There was me and three other girls driven down. I just couldn't believe Styal. I mean it wasn't like Holloway: better, not so prison-like. I didn't have that scaredy feeling. The only time I was really scared was when I went into reception, because they could see I was pregnant but it was all 'Do this, do that', 'Sit down here and take your clothes off', 'Put this dressing gown on.' It was all getting too much for me. I asked, 'Can't I sit down?' They said, 'No. The quicker we get it over and done with, the quicker you can go.' So I said okay, and they took all my particulars down on a card, searched me and everything, then gave me all my things tied up in a bundle. I tried to carry it but I couldn't because of my belly. Actually the screw was all right, she was quite nice because she carried it for me. I was quite shocked. I was taken on the Fox House, the house for pregnant women. It was lucky, really, because I knew a girl there. I got on all right when I was pregnant; everything was great, no trouble, no nothing. Everything was the same, whether you were pregnant or not. I mean we had to scrub floors if we wasn't too far gone, do the cleaning, and education was compulsory. I had to go to education because I was under-age. A lot of girls pulled the trick. They'd say they weren't well and that, so the screws would say, 'Okay then, just do that bit of polishing.'

The day after I arrived there I said I was ill because I did start bleeding. It was the pressure and that. I said to them when I came down, 'I'm bleeding. I might lose the baby.' And all they said was, 'Put on this sanitary towel', but I said, 'No, I'm bleeding quite a lot.' It was a screw called Miss [S]. I didn't like her. She was one of them bitches. No bones about it, just one of them bitches. I stopped my work, and I went upstairs and lay on my bed. You can't do that without permission. Then they did call a nurse over and I was taken to hospital because they thought I was losing the baby. I was escorted to hospital by a couple of screws in an ambulance. Everything was all right and the screws stayed in hospital all night. When I was eight months pregnant they moved me onto Mellanby House. Babies were already there with their mothers. It was just excellent seeing all these little babies in the creche. They were beautiful. I went in there on a Wednesday, and on the Thursday I came into labour. I went to Manchester Royal; two officers came with me and they stayed all the time. On the way I didn't care that they were with me, but afterwards they were there all the time in their uniforms, and everyone knew we were from the prison.

I gave birth to a nice little girl and forty-eight hours after I'd had the baby I had to go back to the prison. They usually let you

stay on. I wasn't a difficult patient – I don't know why I had to
go back.

When you go back you have ten days' rest in bed. There was
one nurse who was really good because I wanted to breastfeed
but I didn't have the patience. She always had time for me and
helped me. She told me, 'You can cope, don't be stupid, you can
do it. Get yourself together.' She was on every day for those ten
days, and there was one screw who came up to see me every day,
even though she was working on a different house. The screws
on Mellanby were a lot nicer than the screws on Fox House.
Most of them were older – I think they were chosen specially.
They used to come into the creche and hold the babies if you
were in the bath or something like that. They were good. We
used to go on exercise and they'd say, 'I'm pushing the baby
round, you're not, I am.' They were just a nice crowd of officers.

I didn't have any visits in Styal. It was too far for them to come
– not that they'd all have wanted to come anyway. It didn't
worry me. I mean, my eldest brother used to write to me like
every single week, and as long as I was getting a letter from
someone I could take it. That's all I needed, one letter a week. I
didn't really bother about all these visits – I mean, I knew it was
just too far for anyone to come. I think visits would have upset
me. I couldn't really have handled it if I'd had any.

I started to get into trouble on Mellanby House. Why should I
be pushed about? Okay, I've done a crime, I'm doing my time.
It's the way they talked to you: 'Come here, go there.' It's not
right. They should call you by your first name. We had to call
them 'Miss'; call them anything else and we were nicked. They
should show a bit more respect for us.

One day we were just coming back from education, there
were six of us. You can't walk on the grass at Styal; you're not
allowed to touch that grass without permission. All my friends
got across, but I put one foot on and – I'm not lying, I'm not
going overboard – one foot and bang, bang, bang on the
window. A screw shouted 'You're nicked.' If you're nicked,
four or five screws come to the house the following day to take
you to Bleak House, the punishment house. So the next day I

stripped the bed, tidied up and that, made my bundle and waited. This was about four months after the baby was born. I was waiting and I wasn't sure whether they were really coming for me or not. It was all a bit of a wind-up. Then I see four screws come up and I thought, 'I'm nicked, I'm nicked.' I was scared, I was really scared. I didn't know how to go about it, you know. A screw called out to me and said, 'Hand me your tobacco tin.' I knew then I was going down to Bleak House.

They take all your clothes off you, and you do a quick twirl with no clothes on, leave your shoes outside the cell door and get left sitting in the cell with just a blanket. When you've settled in, they come round and tell you your charge: 'You've been charged with an offence under such-and-such an act.' I just laughed. For walking on the grass! I couldn't believe it. I lost fourteen days' remission because of that. I thought it was pathetic, and I got put on strict escort. I cried my eyes out, I couldn't believe it. The governor came on the wing at half-past ten for my adjudication and I went in at about 10.45 to see her. I come out, turn right; there was this room with a big glass window and officers standing outside, and I had to stand on this little square carpet with a screw standing on one side and another on the other side, and then I went in and I had to stand on another little mat facing the governor's table with two screws, one on either side of me and two facing me, the governor, the chief and the officer who put me on report. The governor she was a right bitch. She gave me a stripping down. Maybe she thought I could do better for myself, instead of getting caught for petty things like walking across the grass. She said, 'You have been charged, how do you plead, guilty or not guilty?' I had to say guilty, didn't I? I was caught red-handed. 'Guilty, Madam.' She said, 'You just don't do these sort of things. In the rule book it says you do not walk on the grass, you can't stroll around anywhere you want on the prison grounds, you're a prisoner like anyone else.' I said, 'Yes Madam, no Madam', so she said, 'You'll lose fourteen days' remission and be on strict escort for two weeks.' They said, 'Do you want to say anything?' and I said, 'No.' I was in a state of shock. What can you do? So they took me back to my cell on

Bleak House and then they escorted me back to Mellanby. The screws on duty at Mellanby said, 'What did you get?' I told them and one gave me a clap on the head and said, 'You can do better than that.'

During my time there I went to education, looked after the baby and that. That's all there was to do, really: there was feeding times, bath the baby, change the baby. When you were on education there was always one of the mothers looking after the babies, but first you had to make sure your baby's fed, clean, changed and asleep. There was many a time I used to try and get back early, rush into the creche, pick up the baby, thinking, 'Oh, I'm going to get done for this' and put her back. Everyone does it, just to make sure the baby's all right. Sometimes they'd say, 'All right, so she's in there for a couple of minutes, leave her.'

The nurses were always telling you what to do: 'Don't feed your baby that way. Do it this way.' Some people were older, already had three or four kids, so they used to just shrug and think, 'Oh shut up, don't tell me how to bring up my baby.' None of the nurses had any kids. I said, 'This is my baby, I'll do what I want, as long as I'm doing nothing out of order.' It used to make big arguments with the nurses. I decided I'd just keep my nose clean and get on with it, but I got put on report again.

Before we went to bed we had to hand in our tobacco tin, but before we did we'd roll up four or five cigarettes and take a couple of strikes [matches] out. Strictly against the rules, but everyone did it. This girl, Lorraine, she'd go in first, hand her tobacco tin in, then run up one set of stairs, along the landing, run down another, and collect everybody else's roll-ups so that when we went in we had nothing on us. We'd all wait for lights out at ten o'clock and go and get our roll-ups from Lorraine. I always rolled five in an evening to take upstairs with me. One night she only gave me four. I said, 'Where's the other one?' and she said, 'My payment.' I said, 'What are you talking about, your payment?' She said, 'For taking it upstairs for you.' I said, 'Leave it out, I want my fifth one now.' I got hold of her: 'Are you going to give it to me?' She goes, 'No.' So I pushed her.

She automatically belted me back. We got into one big fight – the girls just left us to get on with it. But the babies were in the same room, in their cots, and with the noise they woke up. One of the girls put the light on to make sure the babies were all right and to get them back to sleep and one of the night screws must have seen the light. She came round and we got caught, right in the act of fighting, and both of us got taken down the block. I didn't walk down, no way. They carried me. I said, 'I know I'm ruined but I'm not walking down, I'm going to fight all the way. Last time I was down there I got fourteen days' loss of remission for walking on the grass. I don't know what the hell I'm going to get now for fighting.' The screw on duty said, 'Come on, walk down and tell them your story. You'll be all right.' I said, 'No, I'm not walking down.' Four screws come up and they called Lorraine down. I thought, 'Oooh, I'm not going down.' Another four came up. One of the screws said, 'You're one of them, are you? Going to cause trouble?' So I just looked at her and kissed my teeth at her. I wasn't scared, I was angry.

Eventually I walked out the door with them. They just had my hands gently so I broke free and ran – up to the canteen, round the back and down. Everyone in Fox House and Patterson House was looking out their windows and could see what was going on, and Fox House started banging and shouting, 'Leave her alone, leave her alone, she ain't done nothing.' Fox and Mellanby always stuck together. The people on Mellanby were shouting 'Leave her alone, you bastards, she's got to look after her baby!' The screws finally got me. They twisted my arms up my back and got hold of my legs, and they carried me with my legs touching my bum. I was crying with the pain: I thought they'd broken my arm. When we got to Bleak House they put me down, rang the bell, and then chucked me in and slammed the door. I just lay there crying.

They love it – a bit of excitement, bit of trouble . . . Great! Get the boot in, know what I mean? It's my word against theirs. If someone kicked me and I got a bruise, they'd say to the governor, 'She fell down.' Sneaky, I tell you, sneaky. They'd often put the boot in here or there. They let you get away with nothing, and the bigger the crime the harder they're going to be on you. I was only in for petty burglary and for actual bodily harm and maybe I got the boot for the actual bodily harm, I don't know. They thought they were doing society a favour, but they're just someone there to lock us up, aren't they? Like I say, after that incident with the grass I just didn't care.

The next day I was in front of the governor. She read my charge out. The one who put me on report, honest to God, made it sound as if it was World War III and said, 'There were babies in the room and the babies could have got hurt. Little children were involved, anything could have happened.' So that really went against us. The governor said, 'Have you anything to say?' I said my story. There was an argument upstairs between me and Lorraine. She called me a Black bitch. That's all I could say. I couldn't say anything about the fags because that was against the rules. I said I hit her. The governor said, 'Do you think you've got a right to hit her?' so I said, 'Yes, because she called me a Black bitch.' So the governor says, 'I will not tolerate this nonsense in my prison, especially in the mother and baby house.' So she said, 'Right, you will have fourteen days behind the door [cellular confinement], fourteen days loss of all privileges and seven days loss of remission.' I'd already lost fourteen days for stepping on the grass so I just turned round and said, 'Fuck you, love, just fuck you.' They didn't need to walk me out; I just stormed out and went in my cell.

I wasn't allowed to see the baby so I was expressing my milk. The AG came round every day to check you, and every morning I said, 'I want to see my baby', and they'd say, 'Okay, we'll sort it out', and then they kept saying, 'Yes, you can see the baby, we'll bring the baby down, you can see the baby.' So the nurses would come down for me to express my milk and I'd say, 'Where's my daughter? I want to see my daughter.' They'd say, 'No you are not seeing your daughter.' And I'd say, 'But the AG said I could.' 'I don't care what he said, if we don't want to bring her down, we won't bring her down and at the moment we don't want to bring her down.' So I used to try and go for them right at the door, but the door would be slammed in my face. I was mad, punching the walls, head-butting the walls. I just didn't care. So I had fourteen days down there all on my own, no privileges, no cigarettes, nothing. In the evening they let you out and you go and collect your mattress, two sheets and two blankets. They're in a big sack with the number of the cell, so you know they're yours, then you go into the washroom and have a wash. You could only have a bath once a week, at the weekend. I thought that was pretty disgusting: I was expressing my milk so I had to be clean. So I asked to see the governor and said, 'Can I at least have a bath three times a week, because I'm expressing milk and it's not right for the baby.' She said, 'No, you're the same as everyone else. They can give the baby Cow & Gate milk.' My baby had never touched that milk, and she wasn't used to a bottle. They tried to give it her but she wouldn't have it, she threw it up. I never knew anything about this until I came back up and the girls told me. They tried to force her.

Okay, I had committed a crime and I was being punished. All right, I got into trouble and I got fourteen days down the block – that's okay. But keeping me away from my daughter, particularly when the AG had said I could see her . . . I admit I could have killed. I could have got hold of one of them and lost my head. Women screws make me sick, the heartless bastards. I came out of them fourteen days very bitter – I just didn't want to see my daughter any more. When I did see her and I was told they'd given her Cow & Gate milk, I went mad about that. It got to a point where they wouldn't put me on report no more, because I'd just tell them to fuck off. I'd slag them off in front of their faces, and they couldn't be bothered to put me on report. They knew I'd come back up and there'd be more trouble than ever. I'd come in prepared to do my sentence quietly, but they worked me up and wound me up. Let's put it this way, they made me a worse person than when I went in.

I was seventeen when I came out. I'd done thirteen months and I'd been sentenced to between six months and two years borstal. Towards the end I just kept my head down and tried to get on with it.

My social worker promised me a two-bedroomed house for

me and my daughter when I came out, that's why I got on with my sentence. But when I got out there was no house, no nothing. They just lied. I don't know why. They put me straight into a homeless family unit in Norwich and to me that was just another prison. I just went mad, I tell you. There was no way I could cope in a homeless family unit with my daughter, no way. I wanted my own place. So I just went mad. The baby went into temporary foster care to see if I could get myself together and I couldn't. Then she was adopted.

I had to see my probation officer every day. I used to be down at the pub as soon as it opened and then go to the probation officer drunk as anything – you know, saying, 'Oh, I don't care, I don't care', and she used to say to me, 'You'll go back to prison, you know. You're going about it the right way.' I used to say, 'I don't fucking care.' I said, 'If I go back in, I tell you I just don't care no more.' I was getting into trouble again. There wasn't nothing for me, nothing at all. The only thing there was, was the pub and maybe a fight now and again – there was nothing for me out there. I thought there would have been if I'd had a house for me and my daughter, but I was worse than ever, getting drunk every night, fighting every day. I know I could have got my home together, but no, there was nothing, nothing at all. Just trouble.

I was out of prison a short while. Someone had done a job and they thought it was me, so they come after me. I said I wasn't there and I wasn't, but they took me to the station and tried to charge me, but they couldn't get me on it because I wasn't there. I did do things, but I didn't get caught for them. Then I got done for aiding and abetting in a stabbing. I was with someone who tried to stab someone, but they tried to put it down to me. The charges were attempted murder but then they dropped the charges to GBH.

I'm gay and my girlfriend Sarah used to get beaten up by the girl she was with before she started seeing me. I can't stand things like that, I think it's out of order. She kept hassling Sarah, beating her up when I wasn't around. I'd come back and Sarah would have a black eye or scratches. I was sick of it. One day I was with Sarah and my best friend. I was as drunk as a skunk, and the girl who was hassling Sarah came round and said to Sarah, 'You've got to choose, either her or me.' Sarah chose me, so this girl got up to hit Sarah. I stood up and my friend stabbed the other girl – there was total uproar. I knew I was going down for that. With my record, there was no doubt about it: I got eighteen months for it. The girl who actually done it, she got two years.

I went into Holloway. This time I didn't care. I'd been in the place before, I knew what the runnings were and everything, so I just joined in and found out everything that was going on. I'm game for a laugh. It was all right really. If I got into trouble I knew what it was going to be like, going down the block. I knew it all. Look at it this way, in prison I could look after myself. I go in with the attitude, 'I'm tough and I'm going to survive.' I was in Holloway two days and then they shipped me out. They didn't want me there – I don't know why. I went to Bullwood Hall. It's all right. Like I say, I'm a very lucky person, and I loved Bullwood Hall. I was in trouble every week, doing time down the block. I had a good job on the painting party, which I enjoyed, and the house I was on was brilliant. If someone said, 'Right, I'm not going to do this', the whole house would go along with her, not just one or two. If there was a big fight, everyone would join in. It was just good. I'll be honest, I didn't want to come out of there. When I went in, everyone spoke to me straight away, you know: 'You'll be all right on this house, it's the best.' It was just one big crowd, and everyone started to look up to me, wanted to talk to me, asked me for advice and things like that. I thought, 'This is nice, great. They like me, even in a place like this.' The only thing really wrong was the food. It was disgusting – taters every day. Stodge. Heart-attack food. The custard was like water. I didn't eat properly. I don't care what no one says, it was out of order. I used to go to gym every day. I used to play basketball on a Tuesday night and volleyball on a Thursday night and weight training. The only sport I never took in was netball. Can't do with that. I used to go to the gym whenever I could. It would get you out of your cell, and if you were tense you could take it out on the weights or kick a ball about.

The first time you go to Bullwood Hall you get asked three questions. The first one is, 'How long are you doing?' The second one is, 'What are you in for?' The third one is, 'Are you gay?' So if you go in and say I'm in for such-and-such and I'm doing so much time and no I'm not gay, you're looking for trouble, man. I mean, I went in, right – I don't know why, I just had this attitude – and they asked me these questions and the first two questions I said 'Mind your business', and the third question I said 'Yes, I am, so what!' The girls who asked me the questions became my best friends. Other girls come in and tell them everything – what they are in for and how long they're doing and that. They're going to end up by being a joey, a little run-around, to be used, you know? If I went in and said all that I'd have been a joey. I established my position. I wasn't going to be messed around by nobody or by the screws. That made my time easier, a helluva lot easier.

There was no racism in Bullwood Hall or in Styal, as far as I can remember. Nothing as far as I am concerned. But there are no Black officers in Bullwood Hall – I don't know why. There aren't many anywhere.

I did thirteen months. If you've done twelve months or over you're eligible for parole, and all my mates had their parole. But I never did. I was in trouble every week, every single week. It was just stupid things, but I didn't care. I lost time, gained time. The governor I thought was a right bastard. When I first went in she used to give me some good tellings-off and send me down the block and that. Once when I was in trouble, she called me in and said to me, 'You have a lot up here. Why don't you use it and stop mucking about and getting into trouble and losing time. You've got a lot of influence over them girls.' I used to think, 'Who are you talking to? You're talking to a prisoner, you know.' She treated me as a human being towards the end. She used to sit and talk to me, and I thought that was great. I mean, in the summer time when I was on paint party, I used to go down and make an application to ask if we could have our dungarees rolled up into shorts. She'd say, 'Yeah, okay, that's all right. At least you're thinking of the rest. It's the first time it's been done, that someone's come to ask something like that.' We were just friends. I didn't class her as a governor and she didn't class me as a prisoner. I gained a bit of respect for her and she did for me. I thought that was nice. She did give me a boost. She said, 'Settle down and stop getting into trouble, because you're bright.' When I had to see the Board of Visitors to gain some time back I went in and gave my name and number and they said to me, 'Why do you think you should have time back?' Well, I didn't know what to say, but she stood up and said, 'The reason she wants time back is because her behaviour's got better. She hasn't been in trouble for six months and she's doing really well.' I tell you, if it hadn't been for her I wouldn't have got time back. I was expecting nothing, but I got three weeks.

I wasn't really equipped to do anything on my release. I blame myself for that. It was compulsory education, but I used to go over there and sit and stare out of the window. It was there, it was all there, but I thought, 'No I'm not doing this.' I still to this day want to be a painter and decorator. I learnt all I know in there, and I do a bit of work here and there for people now. That's the only thing I'm interested in, painting and decorating.

I'm gay, as I said. If you're lesbian, so what? If the screws at Bullwood know you are a lesbian, no sweat. But if you've got a girlfriend on the same house they watch you, because they don't want to see any 'lesbian activities' going on. You get nicked straight away. I never had no hassle. I think women should be able to have relationships in prison. A lot of girls tried to have relationships because everyone needs someone to talk to; everyone needs sex, love and attention and all that. I think that should be allowed. At Styal they're literally looking at you all the time. If you're arm-in-arm they'll do you for lesbian activities – you can be put on report for that. And you have no privacy. I couldn't write a letter saying I was depressed, because they'd read it and come and say to me, 'Are you depressed? Why don't you come and talk to me about it?' But you don't want to talk to them, because they'll go and talk to all the other prison officers.

I don't care what no one says, that's the way I see it. I'm not having them chatting about me. No, I never told them anything, nothing at all.

When I left Bullwood Hall I went to a hostel in London. It was okay. I got on great, you know; I was there for six months and then I got a flat with my girlfriend. It's beautiful. But the hostel was great, good crowd. I'm finally settled now. No more trouble for me.

Soon after we spoke to Lee, her relationship with Sarah ended. She moved back into the hostel for a while and has since gone to live in Leicester.

Joanne

Joanne was forty-seven and interviewed while living at a hostel for people who had been sleeping rough on London's Embankment. She described her experience not only of prison but also of life in Rampton, a Special Hospital. Run by the DHSS but staffed by members of the Prison Officers Association, these special hospitals are a mixture of psychiatric hospitals and prisons. Prisoners can be transferred to a special hospital during their sentence if they are felt to be mentally ill and a danger either to others or themselves. A significant number of women are transferred in this way. Once in a 'special', a woman can expect to be there for years rather than months. Release is dependent on the Mental Health Tribunal. Following numerous complaints about brutality in the late 1970s, an investigation was conducted at Rampton and a number of staff members received prison sentences. We had hoped to visit Rampton to gain an up-to-date picture of life there, but were refused access by the Rampton authorities.

In prison, at least you know you've got a date you're going to come out, but in Rampton – the place of no return – you never know when you're going to come out. People say to me, 'You're not good-looking or anything' – people always tell me that, I've got used to it now – 'but,' they says, 'You've got a great personality', because I can mix with anybody, no matter who they are. It's Rampton that messed my life up, I know that.

I was born in Ireland, but I was brought up in London. I can't

154

even remember coming – I always thought I was born here. I lost my mother when I was seventeen. She was only forty-seven. I had been in trouble, but not bad trouble; I'd been a problem child, I think. My mother and father separated so I went to a place in Sevenoaks in Kent run by nuns, like an approved school. I used to run away looking for my father, not stealing or anything, just looking for my father, and my mother used to worry. I've got an older brother and we were very close. All my trouble really started when my mother died. We had to have my mother embalmed because we are Catholics, so I used to go and see her every evening like, and I wouldn't accept she was dead. The only time it hit me was when we went to Ireland for the funeral and, you know, when they're putting the earth over her and I had a complete . . . I don't know. We came back to London, and when we got off the train at Paddington I ran away. I ended up in Tooting Bec psychiatric hospital. I had a breakdown and lost my speech and walk for a while. After I got out of there I went down the West End and I met this bloke, Tommy, who said, 'Would you like some pills.' They were pep pills. So I said, 'Yeah.' I ended up on the game for him, a prostitute.

I got nicked for soliciting. Years ago, when you got nicked for soliciting, you didn't get fines like girls get now. You were sent to prison. I got three months in Holloway. Then one night after that Tommy and me were going home. Tommy had a gun. I had never seen a gun before in my life. The police pulled us. Tommy gave me the gun to hold and of course, me, like a big baby (I was only a baby – well, in my mind), I started going 'Bang, bang' to the coppers, thinking it was a toy. So they took the gun off us and gave me a really bad hiding. I was taken to court and I got eighteen months. Tommy skipped [jumped bail]. They would have given me probation but I refused it because I didn't know about the law then. They explained it to me and said, 'If you break it, you get prison.' So I refused probation and I got eighteen months in prison. I was in Holloway, but it wasn't bad then. I mean, the first thing they'd say to you was, 'You either do it the easy way or the hard way and it's up to you.' I was a bit of a tearaway, but I was all right in there. I came out, and I can't remember how long I was out, but it wasn't all that long (I was eighteen, eighteen and a half), and then I went back in and I think I got a three-year stretch for dipping. You know, taking fellas back and robbing them and that.

When I was young, I thought it was a great thing, going to prison. I thought Holloway was lovely. I was wild, I didn't care about no one. On punishment they were strict, because years ago if you got into trouble there was two male officers working there and they put you on punishment. If they were going to put you in the pads [padded cell], the female screws knew they weren't going to get hurt because the men would put you in. I can remember one day, when I was on bread and water – they don't have it now, three days on and three days off – they came up to fill my bucket and I was in a right temper. There was a male screw standing on the steps. I thought, 'Right, I'll get my own back on you', and I threw the water over him. What upset the officers was the doctor – he said for me to be taken out of there and sent over to the hospital wing. They didn't like that at all. They thought I'd got off too lightly. What they do now, which they wouldn't have allowed years ago, is if you decide to starve yourself they let you. What I find with prison officers is, they've got no heart. All you get out of them is, 'We've got a job to do' and 'If you had any sense you wouldn't get yourself into trouble and end up in here. You'd be like us.' They don't realise it could happen to them. They could go out and get themselves into trouble and they'd be in the same position. They don't understand that.

I used to cut myself to try and get attention, and they've had me in straitjackets for that in Holloway. Sometimes I tried to kill myself, like when I did this scar on my arm. I had a hundred stitches – it goes all the way up, and it was infected as well. I never cut myself on the outside, only in prison. I set my cell on fire because I hate being locked in. I thought if I set my cell on fire they'd let me out – that's what I thought at the time. So, of course, I couldn't have been trying to kill myself, because as soon as I set it on fire I rang the bell. But as I was always getting put in my room and ringing the bell they probably thought, 'Oh, she's messing around again.' When they did come I could have been dead, because the smoke had got to me, I'd flung myself on the bed. They just got me in time, got me off the bed and put me in the hospital wing. I wasn't burnt – they come just in time.

There was a woman in Holloway when I was doing my three-year sentence who used to keep picking on me. I knew I couldn't fight her, no way could I fight her. So I worked out a way of getting her. I got an empty milk bottle (in those days pregnant women in the prison used to get bottles of milk) and I went down to where she was in the workroom. I said, 'Do you want to fight?' She said, 'Yeah.' I said, 'Well, come on then.' So as we walked out of the workroom she grabbed me and I said, 'Not here, the screws will stop us.' I says, 'Let me go upstairs first.' Anyway she came up the stairs and as soon as she got upstairs I broke the bottle (this was when they said I had a brainstorm) and I cut her to pieces. I had done damage to one of her eyes and I'd given her an awful battering and when the screws came to get me I had a go at them as well.

I was taken to court for what I done and the judge cut my sentence because he said I was doing too long for my age. Then I went to see the doctor and was taken out to an army unit and they put this 'perm' on me head [an electroencephalogram – a brain scan]. You know when you get a perm on your head with rollers? Well, it's like that and it's all electric. Then you've got a big thing like a machine and they're firing questions at you. You know on a heart machine you get a line? They kept asking questions and it made a line.

Well, you know, you get mouthy sometimes. I said, 'I'm not answering no more questions, you can bugger off' and all that. Do you know what they certified me as? An abominable aggressive psychopath. I think the doctor got me certified because he didn't agree with my sentence getting cut. One day the doctor sent for me and said, 'You're going to hospital, Joanne.' Well, I was laughing, I thought that was all right. I could discharge myself from hospital. Little did I know I was going to Rampton. On the way there, they had me on Paraldehyde [a major tranquilliser]. So I'm in the car and the driver said, 'Are you all right?' I said, 'Oh, I'm laughing. I'll come and see you tomorrow. I'll be out. I'll discharge myself.' Then I heard him say to them, even though I was drugged up, 'Does she know where she's going? She'll not get out again.' I went mad. I said, 'What do you mean I'll not get out?'

You've got to be certified to go to Rampton because it's for the criminally insane. You go in and you're put in a room for three days – all you've got is a mattress and you don't see anyone except the nurses that bring your food in. After three days I heard someone saying 'court' and I said, 'I want to see the judge.' Well 'court' was what they called exercise! I saw some bad things go on there. I was there two years and never caused no trouble. I was as quiet as anything and they let me out after two years, on licence [supervision by a social worker]. But I stayed out one night and got into trouble: I had an argument with someone, and I was taken back to Rampton. I was back for four years, no court hearing or nothing, just straight back. If it hadn't been for my family I'd still be there.

It was a terrible place. At that time it was all mothers, fathers, daughters and sons who worked there, like a clan. There was no way you could bust it. The nurses were really bad – one girl got killed by them while I was there, they throttled her. Alice her name was. I've seen girls cut themselves like you'd never believe: when they cut theirselves, they cut to kill. A lot used to swallow dessertspoons too, and they're hard things to swallow – I never could. I was walking back from the laundry one day with this girl, just walking along right as rain with her, and all of a sudden – biff, biff, through the window with her head. I'll tell you what, there's girls in there that should never be there. I've seen young girls there, because they've got no people to talk for them, the hidings they'd get . . . They got your hands and bent them down like that; got your legs, bent them up and crossed them and then jumped on them. It hurt right up your spine.

I was upset one day and this nurse called me in the office. She said, 'You're high, Joanne, you'd better go in your room.' Well, all the rooms have got shutters and I don't like being shut in. Anyway, I said, 'I'm not going in', so I called her a pig or something. So, when the sister came down, she called me in. She says, 'Joanne, you're going to have to go in your room and be locked up. You've been insulting to the nurse.' I said, 'I'm not going in my room', and as I walked out I smashed the recess and, of course, my friend jumped in, and the only way they got me and her was they hosepiped us. I don't know where we got the strength from, but no one could stop us. So they got the male nurses over and the hosepipes. If you get blasted with one of them it automatically takes your breath away. So we ended up in the jail – that's what the punishment wing's called. When you're there you get no nightdress, no mattress, you're just in on the floor and you've got this fan buzzing all the time. It'd drive you insane – buzz, buzz. When the doctor does his round they throw a mattress and nightgown in. So one morning I got fed up and decided to complain. The doctor came in and I said, 'Look, doctor. All day long we've got nothing to wear', but nothing changed. At night they'd give you a mattress and like, well, it wasn't a nightdress, it was a horrible cloth thing. I used to see girls over there who used to mess theirselves and rub it all into them just so they could get out of the cell to have a bath. It would drive you mad in the cell. All day we were naked. Not a stitch on. The only time we got anything on was when the doctor was doing his round. Of course I never blamed the doctor because he didn't know what was really going on, and it was a waste of time telling him.

We had to work hard in Rampton. We worked like hell. I didn't get any drugs. They gave me cold turkey, and it's a wonder they didn't kill me. I had been on heroin and cocaine and I was getting weaned off in Holloway, so it wasn't too bad. But when I got to Rampton I didn't get anything at all. All I did get when I was in the 'jail' was Paraldehyde and that leaves great holes in your leg from the injection. It knocks you out straight-away. They don't believe in giving you any help if you've been on drugs – they were kill or cure in there. They put me on one thing, but I refused to take it because when a new medicine comes out the girls and men there are guinea pigs. Do you remember when Largactyl first came out? Girls were taking it and walking round like zombies. So I wouldn't take it because I could see the state of the girls on it.

When Alice got killed, they had reporters and everything in, but when the girls were getting interviewed about it by the police the door was wide open and the screws were outside listening to every word you said. If any girl said anything out of order they knew they were going to cop it when the inspectors went. So they were frightened to say anything. What the nurses used to do – they had a habit of throttling people out with their key chains, trying to control people, frighten them. [All the nurses in Rampton carry key chains and Joanne told us they would put these chains round patients' necks until they lost consciousness.] They throttled her, but they went too far and she died. They tried to cover it up by saying she had an epileptic fit, but she had no fit. Anyway, it took them years to sort it out. After I left Rampton a man from the CID came to talk to me, to ask me about it, and I and some others had to make statements. The only ones they could get statements off was ones that had been released. They said they couldn't get no statements in the hospital, it was like hitting your head against a brick wall. So, the next thing I knew, Rampton was taken to court and it was all in the paper, a big row and everything. There was a sister there, and she was an animal. I think she enjoyed hurting people, because when she was hurting she used to be laughing and that used to sicken me. I'd made statements, so I didn't have to go as a witness to the court. They showed me all the other statements made by the others. Apparently a lot of the staff got prison for it.

When you're in Rampton you never see the outside world. You get a show once a month – they get people in – then you get a dance once a week and you get pictures. You aren't allowed to smoke until ten o'clock in the morning and you're not allowed matches. I've never seen tricks like we did there. You know those thick glasses [spectacles]? Well, we'd put the glasses up to the sun, put the fag next to it and get a light off the sun. If you got caught you were in trouble. All your letters are censored, but this nurse used to get my letters out for me [smuggle them out without censorship]. The doctor used to say, 'Joanne, they're complaining again about the way you are treated.' I said, 'Well, you read all my letters that go out, don't you? They're censored.' They didn't know she was taking them out. She was very good. She left because she couldn't put up with the treatment. They were throttling this girl out one day and she just stood there. This sister said, 'Come and give us a hand or you might as well resign.' So she did resign. They throttled people in front of the other patients. If anyone said anything they'd say, 'You'll get it if you don't shut up.'

After the first year at Rampton, you go in front of an independent tribunal – well, it's supposed to be an independent tribunal, but it's a load of rubbish, because the main one that has any say is the head doctor. Then after that, it's every two years. [Mental Health Tribunals review cases on a regular basis and are responsible for making decisions about release and transfer to ordinary psychiatric hospitals.] My brother or one of my relations always came to see me when I was up there. He came one day when I was up for tribunal and the doctor said, 'Would you be willing to have your sister home, knowing that you've got children in the house?' My brother said, 'Listen, I was brought up with my sister, I know my sister better than you and there's no way she should be here. I'd be willing to take her home now.'

I came out in 1970 and I've never been back. They can't take me back now because I've been reclassified, but I was frightened for a long time of being taken back. That always stuck in my brain because they took me back the first time when I was released on licence. That was one hell of a place. And I still believe that treatment goes on to this day. In there they're frightened to say anything, especially when they've got no one to back them. You get an independent tribunal that comes, but people that go in there have been certified, so whose word are they going to take? They're going to take the doctor's word and the staff's. They're not going to take notice of this person who's round the twist.

When I came out it had all changed where I grew up. I couldn't face people. I went over to the pub one evening, and there was only the landlord and his wife there, and me and my brother, and the landlord was a good friend of my brother. My brother said, 'Go in', and I said, 'No, everyone's looking at me', and I wouldn't go in the pub. It took me ages. He'd say, 'Go to the shop', and I'd say, 'No, I don't want to go to the shop', and eventually he'd go to the shop with me.

I'd been drinking a long time, but it got worse when I came out of Rampton and now my liver has completely gone. The reason I drank was that when you're locked up for that amount of time and you've not seen the outside world you lose your confidence. I always had a fear – even though my brother and my relations drummed it into me: 'They can't take you back' – it still was in the back of my head that they could. So I just used to drink and drink and drink.

I soon got back into trouble. I was taking money in pubs and running out. I used to wear disguises, a lot of different wigs. I got caught one time and they sent me to Moor Court, an open prison. [Moor Court has since been closed.] I'd been there about four months when I ran away. Everyone kept running away and they kept getting caught, so I thought, 'Well, I won't.' I think that's the reason I done it, 'cause everyone else kept getting caught. I knew we'd get seen if we went out of the gate, so me and my mate crawled under a hedge. We hitch-hiked a lift right to Cardiff. This fella who gave us a lift kept saying, 'You're not on the run, are you?' I said, 'What do you mean "on the run"?' He said, 'There's a prison back down the road there.' 'Oh,' I said, 'I don't know anything about prisons, dear.' I thought any minute he was going to stop and we'd have had it, and the sweat was pouring off me. I was out on the run a year. In that year I appeared in court three times and got off, but the third time I was just waiting for my bail to come through and I asked to go to the toilet. And two of the screws from Moor Court were there. As I walked out they said, 'That's Joanne B.' I said, 'No, I'm not Joanne.' I always wear trousers and they came up and said, 'Have you got tattoos on your legs?' and I said, 'Yeah.' So they called me all the names and said, 'You've made fools of us. Three times you've been up in court and you've walked out and you've been on the run.' So I didn't go back to Moor Court, I went to Pucklechurch remand centre and from Pucklechurch I was sent to Styal. Two years I done in Styal.

In Styal it was all right because I'd stopped cutting myself by then and they put me in the kitchen. I enjoyed it there. You have to get up an hour before the others, but it's worth it because you're entitled to a bath every night, instead of one a week. When you go into prison the first thing they say is, 'You can either do it the easy way or the hard way, and the easy way is the best.' When I was young I didn't care about the easy way. As I got older I learnt, you can't outbeat them, there's too many of them. In a jail you can't beat the system, because it'll always get the better of you. I've seen it too many times. I never went on punishment the last time I was at Styal. I nearly got into trouble because they put me on the punishment wing to clean it out and I used to give the girls cigarettes and I got told off about it, but instead of giving me punishment, they put me in the kitchen.

After I got out of Styal, me, this girl and a fella robbed a geezer in Bristol, and we did rob him – that is the truth. But I jumped my bail. The girl and the bloke went to court and the bloke we robbed was there, but the case was thrown out. I gave myself up. Of course I knew the case had been thrown out, but do you know what they did to me after giving myself up? They kept me on remand for three and a half months to get their own satisfaction, because they knew I'd walk out of the court. I was remanded at Pucklechurch, then I went up to court, and the judge gave me a year's suspended. Since then I haven't been in any trouble. That must be five years ago. I've never been back to prison since. I don't want to go back. I didn't enjoy it.

Not long after I left Rampton I met Teddy. That's whose name I carry now. Teddy was the best, he meant a lot to me. We've been all over towns, and he always looked after me, know what I mean? And I couldn't make it out, because every man I've ever known used me. He always stood by me when I went to prison. Anyway, he died in October 1985. No one would help me bury him. He's supposed to have a load of mates and he's got two daughters – he was married before – and they didn't even want to know. In the end St Mary's Hospital buried him. A social worker gave me some clothes to wear. I was in a right state and this fellow came down and said, 'Joanne, I never had any time for Teddy, but I've got time for you, and I respect the way Teddy looked after you.' And he ordered two cars and we buried Teddy up at Kensal Rise. Teddy did look after me, he tried his best. When I was drinking really heavy, he'd say, 'You're not eating, you don't want to live, do you?' And then look who died – him and not me.

After Teddy died I went mad on the drink. I didn't care. I didn't have anywhere to live because we were in bed and breakfast, and Teddy used to claim for me. I just didn't seem to care, and I started hanging round Ladbroke Grove, Westbourne Road. That's when I started begging again – you know, for drink – and sleeping on the doorsteps. Then I came over here, the Embankment. I slept down there for a while, and then someone brought me over to the Festival Hall. I was drinking very, very heavy over that time. I'd just drink myself unconscious. If I'm sober I'm very timid, a bag of nerves. If I'm drunk I'll fight Cassius Clay.

I've got a daughter and she's going to college in Ireland. I'll be forty-seven in February and she'll be seventeen. I had her when I came out of Rampton, because when you're on drugs you've got no sexual feeling, you've got no interest in sex. I took her to Ireland when she was five months old and left her with relatives. She's been there ever since. When I took her I had no intention of leaving her, but I was drinking heavy. They wanted to adopt her but I wouldn't let them – no way. I went over with Teddy two years ago and stayed for six weeks. She didn't get her intelligence from me, she's very intelligent. She's a beautiful girl and she didn't get her looks from me, either. I haven't kept in touch with her since Teddy died, because I haven't bothered with anything. But I'm going to start writing to her again. They spoil her over there. I tell them not to, but they still do it. I don't regret leaving her there now, when I see her, 'cause she's a fine girl. If she'd been over here with me she might have ended up like me, and that's one thing I'm glad of – that she won't end up like me. I didn't really miss her because I was drinking, and when I'm drinking my mind is a blank, just a blank.

I never went back on heroin after I came out of Rampton, but I used to take all sorts before that. I started off on Black Bombers and Purple Hearts. You could buy them in the chemist then, and I was on the needle two and a half years. You feel good in the beginning, but in the end you only take it for the sickness – you don't get no kicks out of it. You ain't got a mind of your own, you don't know if you're coming or going, all you think about is where you're going to get the next fix. The price of a fix down the West End now is wicked. You can pay up to £50 and that's a hell of a lot of money. Then they wonder why these girls keep going in for soliciting. Where else would they get the money for drugs? That was partly why I was on the game, but my pimp had a lot of my money as well – he'd tell me I had to make so much. I used to have lots of regulars, and if I was longer than usual he'd come and knock on the door. If I didn't make enough money, oh, I used to get a hiding. It's a bad life. I've seen girls recently who can't be more than fourteen. You ask and they'll say they're eighteen, but they can't be. You can tell from their little baby faces. It's ridiculous at their age. And I don't blame them, I blame the men. They start them off on the gear and that's it. The pimps, they should get arrested, but they're the ones who seem to get off with it. The girls are frightened to name the pimps because they know they'll get a hiding or get cut up or something.

One thing I really don't agree with about prison is – say young people go into prison. They do their time, then they're let loose when they get out again, they've got nowhere to go. The people who run the prison don't give a hoot. You've done this or that, and you go out the door. Naturally, what are they going to do? They're going to get back into trouble again, because they've got nowhere to go or nothing. I think this should be seen into. I mean, after doing your time, you walk out – all right you're free. It's nice to be free, but you've got nowhere to go. You get a grant, but where's your grant going to go? They'll only pay so much for you to go into bed and breakfast. They've got papers down there now and they'll only pay so much. They say, 'Why do they get themselves in trouble?' I mean, what's that old saying: 'The devil makes work for idle hands'?

A lot of people who hang around at the Festival Hall go in and out of jail all the time – in and out, it's all the same to them. In, out, in, out: it still boils down to the same thing. They've got nowhere to live, just the road, so they're quite happy when they go in because they've got a bed. They don't prefer to be in, but at least they've got a bed. I mean, old people that are really drunkards and are not eating. I've seen people that'll not bother eating, they want the price of a bottle of cider. Know what I mean? The drink'll age them, and sleeping rough.

I've got a fear of being locked up. Altogether I must have done about ten years. I hope to God I never go back. I don't want to. It doesn't prove nothing. I've told you, it just makes people very, very bitter, very bitter.

In the months following our conversation with Joanne, her situation deteriorated rapidly. Although she was still officially staying at the hostel, she started sleeping rough again until her bed-space at the hostel was eventually given to someone else. She lived in a hardboard shack under the Queen Elizabeth Hall on London's South Bank for a while, was drinking heavily and her health was very poor. She has recently been admitted to an alcohol unit outside London.

Sue

Sue was sentenced to life imprisonment for murder. A life sentence is the only sentence a court can impose for murder. It is indeterminate in length and the time a 'lifer' spends in prison depends on her behaviour, the nature of the murder and how 'dangerous' she is perceived to be. Lifers are initially assessed during their first three years and a date is then set for their first parole review, when the case is discussed first by a local committee of prison, probation and lay people at the prison, and then by the national Parole Board. If they recommend release, that decision goes to the Home Secretary, who has the final say. If the board do not decide in favour of release, they will set a date for a further review and may suggest the lifer is moved to another prison. Even when it has been decided that a lifer is to be released, the release process can often take up to two years. Towards the end of that time, the lifer is usually sent to Askham Grange open prison where she can live in a hostel attached to the prison and work in an 'outside' job during the day, returning to the prison hostel at night. She is also allowed home leave to visit her family or friends during her last few months. If anything goes wrong during this time, the release date can be withdrawn and the lifer will find herself back in a secure prison.

After release, she is on 'life licence' for the rest of her life. Initially this means that she is under the supervision of a probation officer who has to submit regular reports to the Home Office. If all goes well, the supervision is usually lifted after three to five years. However, the life licence remains in force and if the lifer is convicted of another offence, or even if her general behaviour is felt to cause concern, she can be recalled to prison. Once recalled, the licence is usually revoked and

167

she has to work her way through the release process again.

The fact that a life sentence is indeterminate is one of the hardest aspects for any lifer to come to terms with. It is simply impossible for her to guess how long she will be in prison, away from children, family and friends. The release process is remote and lengthy; many lifers have to wait a year from the start of the review process until they eventually receive an answer. It may well be a 'knock-back', particularly on the first review. Sue's account clearly illustrates the tension, anguish and frustration this inhumane system creates.

Sue and her friend's former lover were charged with the murder of that friend's husband. She was convicted solely on the evidence of the friend. Sue and many other people, including over 300 women from her area who sent a petition to the Home Secretary, say she is innocent. Sue is divorced and has four children. She admitted in court to having had affairs and living 'an active and healthy life'. Much play was put on these affairs by the prosecution. 'I felt I was dragged through the court and more or less given a life sentence because I had affairs, because to me that's what it boiled down to.' The case took four years to come to trial, during which time Sue met John, the father of her youngest child, Rebecca. They lived in Sue's council house with her three sons. For the last three months before coming to trial Sue was remanded in custody.

Sue's story concentrates mainly on the traumatic separation from her children: Barry (14), Matthew (12), Paul (9) and Rebecca (2) at the time she went to prison. It is clear that for her this was by far the most destructive aspect of the ten and a half years she spent in prison.

'Prison,' you've heard people say, 'I could have done it on my head.' It was a bastard. Don't get me wrong. It's dirty, smelly, all those stupid petty rules, but you can cope with all of that. It's the contact with the outside. The dreadful pain you go through with that, with your kids growing up without you. That you can never forget.

When I was sentenced to life I knew it was a hell of a long time, but you block it. You don't believe it. It's not happening to you. You've got this thumping headache and you're watching it and it's happening to someone else. My friends and relations were in court. People were astonished that I got put away. No one could believe it. My QC saw the clerk of the court and said, 'I just can't believe that, I can't believe they can put someone away with no evidence.' And the clerk said to him, 'You're surprised? You should have seen the judge.' But once the jury has found you guilty, the judge can't do anything. The only sentence for murder is life.

I was taken straight to Holloway, the old Holloway, the castle. I'd already spent four months there on remand so I knew what to expect. They dope you up, so my first few days after the trial were just a blur. I don't really remember anything except talking to a probation officer the day after. Apparently I talked for an hour without stopping. Then I had to see the children. God, that was awful. The probation officer said he would get as many of my family to come up as he could. So Barry, Matthew, Paul, Rebecca, my sister and her husband and John all came up from Southampton. We had a visit in what was called the Ivory Tower. I walked in and they all just sat there. I couldn't believe the change in my little girl. She'd changed so much in four months, it was unbelievable. She was playing with some bricks on the floor, and she looked up, like a child would, and looked down, and carried on playing. Then she jammed her finger in something and she ran to my sister and said, 'Mummy', and cried. My sister said, 'No, this is Mummy.' And she came and looked at me. I'll never forget the look on her face. Something registered. By the end of the visit she was coming to me and bringing me bricks and things, but to start with she didn't know me from Adam. Years later, Roger [Sue's probation officer] said to me, 'Did you see Paul's face?' and I said, 'No.' He said, 'Perhaps it's best you didn't. I'll never forget the look on that boy's face.' He was nine years old.

After that first visit we were only allowed a welfare visit [arranged by the probation officer] once every three weeks. They didn't have prison officers in on these visits. The probation officer conducted them. He'd say, 'You just carry on. Try to make it as much a family visit as you can. The room is yours, get down and play with them, whatever you want. I'll sit in the corner. You forget I'm even there.' We've always been very close, the boys and I. We still are. But it was as though they were frightened to speak because they knew where they were. There was always that gap. They didn't feel they could rush up and cuddle me like they used to, it was very painful. During this time, my appeal was all going on. So I hadn't accepted the sentence. I was thinking, 'This is just a nightmare. I'll wake up and it will all be over.' You don't accept it. You can't.

I was in Holloway eight weeks and then they shipped me off to Durham. That was in 1975. Nothing can prepare you for Durham, it's like a different world. I think when they opened H Wing they thought they were going to fill it with major criminals, IRA and whatever. But there weren't enough of them so they put lifers in there, and when they ran out of those they put others in.

The only way I've ever been able to describe Durham is like a submarine – I've never been in one but I imagine that's what it's like. You couldn't see daylight. It felt like you were buried alive. That was your life in there. It was as if the world outside didn't exist. If I stood on my bed and looked out of the window with its four sets of bars, all I could see was a big high wall with a tiny bit of tree over the top. We used to climb on the sink unit in the bathroom and look through a little window so you could see far away the hills and sometimes you'd see a little tiny car going along them. You really felt the need to see the outside world sometimes, just to make sure it was still there. When you went out on exercise it was just in a concrete yard with a wire fence round it, no trees, no grass. There were dogs and male officers patrolling with walkie-talkies around the outside and the inside. Four cameras watching you, following you. All you could see were brick walls. The men from the men's part of the prison had their cells overlooking the yard. They'd shout remarks as we walked round. Sometimes they could be very abusive.

In Durham you weren't allowed to think for yourself, you couldn't do anything. Everything you did was monitored, you couldn't get away from it. When I first went there, there wasn't even classes. We used to spend our time playing cards, though normally you're not allowed to, because of gambling. It was a life-saver, it kept our brains alive. There was little else – washing floors with a green pad and a bar of soap all day doesn't stretch your mind. We weren't supposed to talk whilst we were scrubbing so we used to sing. They used to shout at us to stop. At Durham you had your own room. You were locked in at eight at night until eight the following morning. Once you got over all the bolts and bars and the doors being electronically locked, you could do your own thing: you could sit and cry, write your letters, be close to your thoughts. For me that was very important. Everyone needs their own little space. I couldn't think about my sentence. Every time I thought of it, I dismissed it. I don't think any lifer accepts it. They say most lifers have an outburst of some sort at six months – they don't usually cut their wrists or anything like that, but they scream and smash up, or go right down hill. I didn't think about it. I did, but I didn't, if you see what I mean. I had to cope with Durham. It was so alien – I was too busy trying to cope with the place, trying to survive the place, I couldn't allow myself to think of my sentence. I used though to wake up with nightmares and I'd be crying and everything – I'd wake up and think, 'God, where am I?' It's horrible. You realise where you are and you're on your own. You can't describe it, it's an awful feeling, but there's something inside you that keeps you going.

It was a year before I was able to see the children, and I had to fight to see them. The Social Security wouldn't pay for John and the children to come and see me – they said it was too far, too expensive – so I had to apply to go back to Holloway for visits. [The DHSS will normally pay the travelling costs and overnight accommodation for one visit per month for one relative and the prisoner's children. As Sue's family lived on the south coast, more than 350 miles from Durham, the DHSS said it would be too expensive and would not pay. She had to apply to the Home Office to go to Holloway.] Well, it was unheard of. 'Oh no, you can't go.' Eventually they did agree and I was taken back to Holloway. I can't remember how long I stayed, but it was a very short time. We had three or four very quick visits, and then I went back north again.

Then the appeal came up, and all our hopes were raised, but the Appeal Court said that I didn't have sufficient grounds and they dismissed it. During that year Roger, the probation officer from Holloway, went and spent the weekend in my house with John and the children and explained to them that I was probably going to be away for nine years or more. In the two years I spent at Durham I only went back twice to have visits with the children.

After two years in Durham they sent me to Styal. I still hadn't accepted that I was going to do that many years in prison. You don't, you can't. I had those terrible nightmares for weeks and weeks – well years. We had a psychiatrist at Styal. Several of us used to go and see him just to get Thursday afternoon off. He used to bring in bags of sweets. We'd just sit and talk; it was an afternoon's escape. All lifers could go. I didn't need a psychiatrist but I did need to talk to someone and I did need an afternoon off. He used to say, 'When you have these nightmares, Sue, write them down.' So I wrote them down and he used to analyse them and he'd say, 'It's the guilt you're feeling at leaving the children to fend for themselves. No one has ever said you're not a good mother, but you just can't forgive yourself for leaving them.' You would have thought that if I had killed someone I would have had nightmares about that.

I remember when I first went to Styal, it was on a Friday. They put me on a mixed house [short- and long-term prisoners]. The officer who was middle-aged and quite sweet came up to me on the Sunday evening and said, 'You can go out and walk round the house.' I was only in Durham for two years, but it hadn't even occurred to me that I could now walk downstairs and go outside. In Durham you think there is no outside. You condition yourself to it. She said, 'You've been up there since Friday and you haven't attempted to walk out the door.' She said it upset her. All the girls were in and out, but it hadn't occurred to me to do the same, until she pointed it out.

There were twenty-two women on my house; about six were

lifers, including me. All the rest were long termers and a few were short termers. We were a great bunch. We had some great times. But Styal was so petty. You lost a day's pay for picking a flower or walking on the grass. You had all this beautiful grass and you couldn't walk or sit on it; you had to take a hard chair out and sit on that. Is that a mind-blower or not? I had to go into a dorm when I first went there. Going from a single room where I'd spent two years to a dorm was awful – the noise was terrible. And there were loads of petty things like getting up every morning, even Saturday and Sunday, and having to strip your bed and wash the floor before you could even have a cup of tea. Styal was very hard in many respects, very hard. They were always telling you that you had no rights. Even the governor would say, 'You've got no rights,' so all the time you looked for challenges. It didn't matter what it was – nothing violent or anything like that – but anything that was a challenge you took up.

As soon as I got there I started to fight again for visits. You see, each prison works separately. I think I was at Styal nine months before I got back to Holloway for my first visit. The Social said again there was no way they would pay for John and the four children to come to me. I had to be brought back. The answer came back from the Home Office saying, 'Yes, she will be returned to Holloway every six months for accumulated visits.' You're entitled to one welfare visit a month, so for six months you'd save up and have six visits in two weeks. Roger used to have to organise it all. The prison won't tell you you're going until almost the day before, in case you plan an escape. So you have little time to let your family know. I used to rush a letter off to Roger to say that I was coming. He then had to get in touch with the Social, who had to arrange tickets for them all to get up to London. He was always in hot water with them because he didn't give them enough time. Then, the night before I was due to go, the prison might say, 'Oh, the escort's off, we haven't got enough officers. You're not going until next week.' So I would have to cancel it. This is how it went on.

Then I would get down there, and the children would come

up, and then Social would say, 'Oh, you're only entitled to one visit.' They couldn't get it together that I was entitled to more. I used to be ill before I went down. I used to smoke cigarettes, I used to be sick, had diarrhoea, on and off the toilet. Then I would go on a visit. Imagine what it was like. I used to sit there, and all of them would want to tell me six months' news. I had to listen to three conversations, Rebecca would want me to read her a book or play games, and the boys wanted to tell me everything. Oh God. It was all totally wrong. They say that if you get yourself into prison, you have to suffer. Okay, I was suffering, but the children didn't have to. I think they went through hell. In lots of ways they went through it worse than me. When the visit was over I'd have a thumping headache, my stomach would be knotted up, there'd be hours of agony. The only way I can describe it is like falling in love and it falls apart and you've got this bloody great lump inside you and you don't know what to do with yourself.

After the visits I'd think it was so painful, seeing the children and then coming away from them again, telling yourself that it would be six or nine months before you'd see them again. It was so painful that I used to have to try and cut them out of my life for that time. I wrote to them every week, but it was as if I was writing to – I don't know how to explain it – I had to push them away from me, because I couldn't survive any other way. I knew if I went under I was gone. I wasn't going to get through, it was pulling me down. It was eating my inside away, I didn't know how to stop it. If I'd been in a prison close enough to see them once a fortnight, just one of them once a fortnight, it would have made such a difference.

People say, 'Why did you get there in the first place then?' Well, if I was someone who thieved or someone who went back and went back and went back, well yes they would have the right to say that to me. But no one had the right to say that to me.

That went on for seven years. And every time I came back from Holloway they'd say, 'You look ill.' Of course I did. I don't think they realised how traumatic it was, Rebecca screaming when they had to take her out. It even got to the point where I was going to stop seeing them. I said I couldn't put them through that. Also it is so chaotic in Holloway. I've had visitors there and they've been at the prison for an hour before they've even come and got me.

We had welfare visits in the church. And then other people were using welfare visits for smuggling things in. I got angry over that. I said, 'I never use my children. If I want to fiddle, I'll do it on my own.' I would never involve my children. I said, 'I go down there to see my children and that's all. If you want to strip search me, then you do it. But don't ever say that my family would bring anything in to me, or that I would ask them to.' Then they started telling me that I had to have the visits in the normal visiting room: 'No more welfare visits, you have the visiting hall the same as anyone else.' So my children would come up and they only allowed them half an hour, instead of the hour and a half for accumulated visits. They even made one child wait outside. I went to the governor. I screamed at her, I said, 'I'm not a violent person, but my mouth is my weapon. If I think I'm right you'll hear it.' I said, 'You let me have my four children in on my visit. Not just three. If I had sixteen children I would want to see them all in one go.' This went on for seven years. I got worse and worse. The governor at Styal called me into her office one day and she said, 'Why don't you settle down, Sue, and do your life sentence? Why don't you be easy on yourself? You're eating your insides away.' I mean, I had three major operations while I was in prison, and they reckon it was all down to stress. She said, 'You've brought it all on yourself.' I was fighting a battle all the time. I've always said that if anyone touched any of my children then, yes, I might kill, because my children are my world. Men have done terrible things to me and I've never wanted to kill them. But if anyone touched any of my children – if it's in me, then it would come out. I felt all the time they were doing this they were hurting my kids.

When I went to Holloway from Durham and Styal for the visits, I would ask for a particular cell. The officers would ask why I wanted that cell, and I said, 'Because I can see people in the street.' They thought I was really strange. 'Doesn't it upset you?' I said, 'No, oh no. I need it.' I could see people getting on and off buses and walking in and out of the pub. I just used to sit there with the lights off and watch the buses and the cars and people going up and down the road. I didn't care if they locked me up twenty-four hours a day. I had that to watch.

After a while things started deteriorating at home, mostly through lack of money. The boys were all living with John, and then Rebecca, who had been with my sister, also went to live with him, so he had the four kids to look after. It wasn't easy for him. On one of the visits I remember I said to John, 'Look, I'm not stupid. I'm in here, I don't expect you to be a saint. I know looking after children for a woman is hard enough, it's doubly hard for a man.' I said to him, 'Go out and enjoy yourself. I understand all that. Just please, please, don't hurt my kids.' But he couldn't manage. He couldn't keep his head above water, and nobody would help. He had to give up his job to look after them. And then from what I understand he was on the verge of a nervous breakdown. The authorities just didn't want to know. Roger said, 'If we'd sent all the boys to your sister's, she would have been made the legal guardian and she would have got something like £45 a week each to keep them.' But they wouldn't do that with John. I don't know the exact details of it. They weren't his children, you see. You can't live on air. Three boys at school, needing shoes every six weeks. Then things started to get nasty. Matthew left home. He was sixteen by this time. He didn't say anything to me. That's how marvellous they are. As young as they were, they didn't tell me. A lot of it I didn't actually know until I came home. If I had known in there, I think I would have committed suicide. The kids were absolute bricks, they really were.

So Matthew left and went to live with Grandpa – that's their father's father. I had divorced my husband and from the day I got sentenced he disowned them. He was no father to them, but then he wasn't before anyway. I didn't know there was any animosity. I just thought Matthew preferred to live with Grandpa. Then things went on and John used to come and see me with the kids and Rebecca used to say things like, 'Joy said this, Joy said that.' John would immediately say, 'Oh, that's, er, um, her playschool teacher.' I was putting two and two together. But it didn't matter. It did hurt a little, but it didn't matter. All I wanted was that they were kept together – that was the priority. The rest I had to accept. I thought if he was happy in whatever he was doing, he'd be more content looking after them. It's common sense. Things started to break down, though. He was obviously seeing this woman. He used to make the two boys come home from school – I didn't know any of this until I got home – and do the housework and then cook their own meal, and then look after Rebecca while he went out, and apparently not come home all night. Of course the boys wanted to be out in the evenings with their friends.

Then one day the welfare at Styal got a phone call and called me over. They said, 'Matthew said he will be up tomorrow.' I said, 'What?' They said something had happened, not to worry. All he said was, 'Tell my mum I will be there tomorrow.' He came up and said, 'Well, mum, John threw Paul out last night.' Paul was just thirteen. Apparently he had gone out with his friends and had been told to be in by a certain time because they were babysitting and John was going out, but Paul came in at nine instead of seven. He said to John, 'I've fallen off the boxes at the supermarket and hurt my arm.' And John apparently said, 'Get up to bed, you're not having anything to eat.' And Paul said, 'I don't know why you don't put me in a home, I'd be happier.' Barry heard all the screaming and shouting and went downstairs – he's told me since that he had to jump in between them. John threw Paul out there and then and he went to Grandpa's, which isn't that far away, but it was eleven o'clock at night. Matthew told me he had to send Paul to hospital because he'd hurt his arm and there they found it was broken. Barry left John that night as well. My sister said he could stay with her – she has two boys – but Barry didn't want to go there. He was old enough to look after himself. So Matthew stayed with Grandpa; Paul with my sister, who was made his legal guardian. So that left John with just Rebecca. Barry went to live with a girl he was seeing. Then the two of them went and lived in a beach hut for six months. They gradually moved round and round. He went through a rough time. When he left school he did an apprenticeship in bricklaying, but he was also going to college and wanted to get on there. But when they lived in this beach hut it was too far to get to college, so he just let it go, which was a terrible shame. Now he's gone back to college and is doing very well.

A few weeks after one of the visits with John and the children, Roger came up to Styal. He told me John wasn't going to visit me anymore. I thought, 'Well, I knew it was coming', I just didn't know when. So after that Roger used to bring the children up for the accumulated visits until the boys were old enough to come on their own with Rebecca. They were all split up in different places. They were marvellous, really marvellous.

When I was in Styal the idea was put forward of having a caravan in the grounds so that those of us who were doing very long sentences could see our kids for a weekend. The screws threatened to walk out if it came about; they said the girls would use it to have drugs brought in. They also said, 'Why should you have your old man in and have sex?' Oh, I got so upset, so angry. I said, 'I don't want that. All I want is to cuddle my kids without you people watching.' We'd had our children taken away from us and they had us taken away from them. Then people say, 'You should have thought of that.' How can people be so stupid?

I remember when I'd just done three years, I still hadn't accepted it. I was still going along thinking something was going to happen. And then I remember one day I got up and thought, 'Oh God, three years.' And it seemed like an eternity. That was when I said to myself, 'If you're going to do a life sentence you have another six years. At least.' I can remember being so down, thinking, 'Oh God, how am I going to get through six more.' An officer said to me once, 'All you lifers follow the same pattern. It's almost as if the day you're given your sentence your mind goes to sleep. You cope with traumas and everything, you do everything automated, and then one day you wake up.'

So I started setting myself targets, like never to look at clocks. And when it's meal times, never say, 'What's the time?' Don't even look at the days. Look at months. In fact, look at this time next year. So I started doing that: 'By this time next year I've got to have knitted twelve Aran jumpers.' That was one thing. And then when I finished that, on to the next thing. Every time I finished a task, I set myself another one. Even when I went to work each day, I set myself a task. I worked in the machine room making shirts. I'm a dressmaker by trade.

In Styal they make up the rules as they go along. You never knew where you were: today it's a rule, tomorrow it isn't. It was all so petty, so unnecessary. The only way I could survive was to fight it. If I didn't I would have gone under; that was the way I got through. If I thought something was wrong, I'd argue to the end.

At Durham life sentence prisoners had certain privileges. You were allowed your own cup and saucer and your own teapot, a teaspoon, cassette player, things like that – a few things that short termers weren't allowed. I was led to believe they came with your sentence, but when I went to Styal they said you had to earn your privileges through good behaviour. I remember once a girl had some Rive Gauche perfume. I don't know where she found it. It was like gold dust. You're not allowed perfumes or anything like that – all you smell normally is sweaty bodies, and it doesn't matter how much soap they use to scrub it, it's always there. No fresh air. The officers on the house started to say, 'Some of you girls smell very nice.' Then one day they found it, so the whole house lost their privileges for three weeks. We lost our radios, our spoons, our cup and saucer, everything. Shit, let them take it! We wouldn't give in, we wouldn't tell them where we'd got it.

As I said, Styal was hard, very hard in many ways. It didn't matter how long you'd been there – six months or six years – there were no concessions. For instance, one day I went down the workroom to go to work. I was in my fourth year. And my friend Helen was on a hunger strike, trying to get home leave, because although it was a statutory thing, you didn't get it in Styal. Helen was determined to get this home leave, so she starved herself for forty days. You should have seen her – she used to have to walk around holding her trousers up because they were miles too big. They wouldn't let her have a belt because they said she might hang herself. Anyway, if you want to go to the toilet you have to ask, and if there's anybody in the toilet you can't go, you have to wait for them to come out, in case there's LA [lesbian activities] going on in there. I'd say, 'If I want an affair with a woman I'll have one, and there's nothing you or anybody else can say. I got a life sentence and the judge didn't say that I wasn't to have an affair with another woman.' So anyway, I saw Helen go in to the toilet, and God she was ill. Well, I didn't even think, I just went in there. Just before you go into the actual toilets there's two buckets for the cleaners, and we were sat on these upturned buckets, and I'm trying to talk some sense into her. I said, 'Look, they're not going to give in, you're going to kill yourself. They will not give in.' Well, all of a sudden the door burst open. We knew we weren't supposed to be in there together so the two of us got up and ran into the toilet, which is the usual thing you used to do at school. Well, the supervisor came and pushed the door open and we were both stood there. She said, 'Out.' So out we walked. She said, 'I'm disgusted with the two of you.' Well, when she said that everybody thought there was something going on. 'Especially you, Sue, I'm ashamed of you' – not ashamed because she'd seen anything, it just wasn't my normal behaviour. We were told to go back to our machines. Suddenly, the supervisor says, 'Sue, come here.' And as I passed Helen's machine she said, 'You're going to the block.' I said, 'Oh shit.' I had three illegal letters on me. That was another thing you used to do, you see. All these girls in prison, they write letters to each other. Again it's to keep their brains alive more than anything. They write and tell each other that they love them. Well, of course they do – when people are that lonely, loving someone is so important. I had a friend in there, and we used to just sit and cuddle each other – no lesbian affair was going on between us, but we cuddled each other because that was so important, someone to put their arms round you. Specially when you've just started a sentence. Helen was gay. And I found her a very good friend, I thought the world of her. The fact that she was gay just didn't matter, she was my friend. So, anyway, I had these letters on me that I was going to give out in the workroom to different girls. I thought, Oh my God, what to do with them? If I drop them – the officer that came to send me to the block was pretty keen – she'd hear them fall. So what do I do? Eat them.' I put them in my mouth, and I was chewing away – one, two – and they wouldn't go. We got to the door, and I just swallowed. Well, it was so painful when I swallowed those letters. The officer said, 'Strip'. I said, 'You want my clothes off, you take them off.' Because I got like that and because I wouldn't take my clothes off, they didn't search me. I was so sick I sat there with this bloody great lump in my chest.

I was given twenty-one days behind the door for being absent from my seat without leave and for being in the toilet with another inmate. I was put in a cell with no windows. If there's fight in you, that's when it comes out. In the morning they come in and wake you up at half-past six by kicking the door open: 'Up!' They take the mattress away, and you sit on the wire spring all day. You get half an hour exercise, and you're given a religious book or the Bible. Nothing else. You have a plastic bowl for washing in – they give you lukewarm water in the morning – and you strip wash with that and then you have to wash your floor with it. There's no toilet in the cell, you have to use a potty. So I used to ring my bell: 'I want to go to the toilet.' 'You've got a pot.' I said, 'Oh no.' There was an East Ender in Durham, she'd been in prison many times. She knew the rules inside out, she was lovely. She said, 'You're not going to get through a life sentence until you learn to turn round to someone and say "Fuck off." ' I said, 'Oh, I couldn't.' She said, 'You will.' Well, I mean, before I went to prison I used to say, 'Oh bugger it' and think *that* was awful! She said, 'I'll tell you the rules. We all learn them. If you ring to go to the toilet and they tell you to use your potty, you say, "No, you're on duty, and if you're not busy you've got to let me out to the toilet".' And I did that, I wouldn't give in. And I think that's when my haemorrhoids, which I'd had since Rebecca was born, got so bad, because I wouldn't give in. That's what made them worse.

One day when I was down there I'm sat in my cell and the door opened. It was one o'clock. 'You're going to hospital at half-past one.' I had an appointment for my haemorrhoids. 'I'm bloody well not,' I said. 'You've got to give me six hours notice.' I always came up with something, I always fought them. I said, 'If I've got an appointment with this surgeon I want a bath, I want to wash my hair, I want clean clothes.' And in an hour and a half I'd had it all. The doctor in the hospital knew I was in prison. He said, 'Right, now I want to try something on you, I want to tie them off. It will be very painful.' Well, if they say it's going to be painful you know it's going to be. He said, 'But I will give you painkillers.' I said, 'Hang on a minute. I'm in prison. We don't have painkillers. Unless you give me a letter they won't give me anything.' He said, 'I'll give you a letter, but are you willing to have it done?' I said, 'Yes, but I'm in the punishment block.' He asked what I was in there for. Well, he obviously didn't believe me when I told him, because outsiders wouldn't, so he went out and asked the officer. Afterwards she said, 'You embarrassed me, telling him why you were on the block.' He tied off my haemorrhoids and I was sent back to prison and the block. This was on Friday. From then till the Monday morning I never had a thing – no painkillers, nothing. He'd written a letter to the prison and put the doctor's name on the envelope, but because that doctor wasn't in until Monday morning, I wasn't given any medication at all. By Monday morning – well, I was grey. I was ready to commit suicide. I didn't know where to put myself. It got to the point that I was going to put my hand up inside and pull whatever it was out – he said he'd put a ring up there and that it gradually dissolves. I walked that cell all night.

The doctor does his rounds on Monday morning. He walks by the cells, the doors are open and he says, 'Good morning, you all right? Thank you.' And before you can answer he's gone on to the next one. Well, this time when he came I was leaning on the wash stand. He looked at me, he walked past, came back and said, 'You all right?', and he saw my face. I said, 'No I am not.' He said, 'Get this woman's notes, Sister.' He opened it and saw

this letter and said, 'Good God. You ought to have had a –
whatever-they-called-it. Get her up to the surgery straight
away.' Well, all hell let loose. They sent an officer to get me,
because you go everywhere with an escort. On the way up to the
surgery she said, 'Sue, what they've done to you is unforgiv-
able. Do you want me to do anything?' I said, 'No. Thank you,
but no.' I went up there and the doctor examined me and said,
'Well, you're over the worst of it.' I said, 'Don't I bloody know
it.' He put me on painkillers, and medicine. He said, 'They
won't let you up from the block, but I'll make sure you've got
your mattress and a blanket, so you can sleep.' I just laid on my
bed and slept.

During my ten and a half years I also had a hysterectomy and
my gall bladder out. The hysterectomy – I'd had some trouble
in that area before I went inside; prison just speeded it up. Lots
of women had hysterectomies, especially in Durham. With my
gall bladder, I kept on having all these terrible pains. The doctor
at Styal said it was indigestion, but when I went to Cookham
Wood the doctor there said it was my gall bladder. It was too late
to do anything about it, so I had to have it out.

After my twenty-one days down the block I returned to my
house. I stayed on that for three years, then I was moved on to
the lifers' house. There were nine of us at that time but we were
only there for a short time before they closed it and opened
another one for sixteen. In the lifers' house you had your own
room. I very rarely watched television because everyone used to
sit in the sitting room, and unless it was something that was
really absorbing I wanted to scream and run out. To me they all
looked – I can't say they'd accepted it, but they were sitting
there as if that was the end of it, like old ladies in an old people's
home. Sitting there waiting for the end. So I just sat upstairs in
my own little room. My radio was my lifeline. I'd sit and I'd
never stop knitting or doing handicrafts, the whole time I was in
there. If I had one shilling for every jumper I've knitted . . .
Often the officers would come up, and say, 'Come downstairs',
and I'd say, 'No, I'm quite happy', and I was. I spoke my mind
but I had to do it my way – go to work, work bloody hard, go

back to my house. I'd have my bath, get changed into something comfy, have my tea, then sit in my little room. Unless I said to someone, 'Come in', they couldn't; it was my sanctuary. In the lifers' house you respected each other. If you were invited to someone's room you went, but you didn't go uninvited.

I worked in the workroom for four and a half years. I would like to have done full-time education but lifers are relatively poor and in the workshop I could earn £3 a week. It would have been half that if I'd done education. With £3 a week I could save up and then when I went to see the kids I could take them a big bag of sweets. I could also afford to buy balls of wool to knit them sweaters, and in that way I was still doing my bit as a mum. But after four and a half years I couldn't go back in the workroom any more. I was saturated with it. I couldn't stand it any longer. So I asked to go on the gardens. I didn't care if I didn't get any money. I had to have peace and quiet.

I stepped into a different world. I worked in the gardens and then the greenhouse. It was like someone being given back their sight. I loved every single second – I couldn't get enough of it. It was feeding me. I used to go there in the morning, rushing in to pick the things up and look at the little seedlings coming through, see to the plants. It was my baby. I had something to care for, to look after. I loved it. The fella I was under, the instructor, he was a nice bloke, he really was a lovely person. He was a civilian worker and he'd tell me things he was doing at home. It was a bit of the outside. He used to share his bacon sandwiches with me every morning at break time and we'd just sit and talk. He was a really peaceful man. He could see I was in a state and he took great pains to slow me down. He was the best medicine I'd had in years. I really trusted him. I really looked forward to going. Then one day they came in the greenhouse and said, 'You're moving, Sue', and they put me over on the Centre [prison officers' office] making tea. They thought there was something going on in the greenhouse. My friend Sally said, 'You know what you did wrong? You walked to work smiling. You looked happy.' You see, I was, I was happy. I used to walk round that greenhouse singing. I would have stayed up there twenty-four hours a day, but because I was happy they thought I was up to no good. Knocking it off with him in the greenhouse. That's the way their minds work. He brought the outside in to me and made me live again and that's what Sally said: 'You came alive again, Sue.' That's when you're dangerous.

I didn't like the job on the Centre. I said, 'You can stick your job up your arse because I don't want it.' I had to make their tea, their toasted sandwiches, clean up after them. You'd hear them discussing who was going to get found guilty on report and what punishment they were going to give them before the poor bastards had even been before them. To me that was a red rag to a bull. As soon as I started there I began to get quite ill: they said it was a put-up job. I kept getting diarrhoea and stomach pains, but it was my gall bladder.

At seven and a half years I was eligible for my first parole review, but in 1980, after I'd done five years, my QC and barrister took my case to the Home Office and spoke to Leon Brittan, the Home Secretary at the time. My MP had also taken up my case. They said, 'He won't pardon you, but there is a possibility he will release you on parole.' You can imagine what I felt like. The AG at Styal did an assessment of me, it went off, and I waited and I waited and I waited. My QC was as certain I was going to get it as he was certain I would walk out of the trial a free woman. I didn't get it. I never found out what happened. They never give you reasons.

So I went up at seven and a half years. No lifer expects her first parole, but what you hope for is a date for a review. They're doing reports on you all the time and every year you have to see the governor and the chaplain – everyone looks at you. Anyway, mine went up. Normally they would call you up at 1.30 to tell you whether you'd got parole or not. I said to them [the prison staff], 'Don't send for me on the 1.30 call-up. I won't go.' It was always the same time so all the women in the house knew and would be waiting for you as you came back. So there I am, working away, and all of a sudden: 'Sue go to . . .' My thought is, 'Oh God, it's the children.' So I went flying up. This was half-past nine in the morning. I sat down, the AG was there.

He'd read it before I realised what it was, because I expected him to say something about the kids. He said, 'Do you want me to read it again?' and I said, 'Yes. Say that bit again.' And it was the usual thing, you know: 'The Home Office have not seen fit to release you on parole, etc., etc., you will be transferred immediately to Cookham Wood prison. A year from now you will be up for parole again.' So I got a year's review – again no reason was given. I didn't ask, it's a foregone conclusion that you're refused the first. Really all you looked for was the review and mine was a year, which was a good result.

I spent two years in Cookham Wood and then I was sent to Askham Grange for the last seven months of my sentence. I got my first home leave soon after I went to Askham. I was very nervous. I caught the train in York to King's Cross, where Roger met me. We phoned the boys and then caught the train to Southampton, where the boys and Rebecca were waiting for me. The journey was quite easy really. I remember wanting a drink on the train but I was too nervous in case I got the money wrong. Other lifers were the same. We always ended up with a purse full of change because we gave £1 coins whenever possible. My family were fantastic, we had a wonderful weekend. After that I went home once every month or six weeks. The last few times I did the whole journey myself. One thing I was determined to do was conquer the underground in London.

I spent all the seven months at Askham in the hostel, except for two weeks. From there you're sent out of the prison to work. To begin with I found it very difficult. I was terribly nervous. Everything had changed so much. I wasn't used to traffic, the noise, men, money. I was waitressing in a Happy Eater Restaurant. Everyone was very nice – the people I worked with all knew about me so I didn't have to live a lie. They used to say, 'I don't believe it.' It's true, people have this idea we're all monsters.

I did find relating to men a problem. I still do. I'm all right if someone else is there, but not on my own. All the time you're in prison the officers are watching you, especially if you're working near a man, because they think that's the one thing you're desperate for. Believe you me, it was the last thing on my mind! I find I still cannot be alone with a man. It doesn't really matter, because I'm not interested. Before, I used to live a 'healthy active life', but now it's gone, they killed it a long time ago. To be dragged through the court and more or less given a life sentence because I had affairs, and then to be constantly told for ten years that even to go near a woman is disgusting . . . The simple act of linking arms as we walked down the avenues was scorned. How can one be expected to return to a 'normal healthy life' after ten and a half years' indoctrination in this way?

When I first went inside and saw lifers I used to think, 'How can they laugh and joke, even have girlfriends when they have kids outside. Why aren't they sitting crying?' It used to tear me up inside. But as you go on through it you understand. You have to make a life for yourself, cut off the outside – you couldn't manage otherwise. When you come out you think, 'I'm going home and everything's going to be like it was', but of course it's not, because all those years have been pushed apart and it's all got to come back. They're there, all my family, they all live in that little radius where I am. I could go to any of them, they come to me, but . . .

I must have got institutionalised. When I was in there some of the women used to come back sentenced again, and I would think, 'Good God, fancy coming back. What are they thinking of?' I've heard people say, 'I was so lonely out there.' I couldn't understand. Now I do, and so does my friend Sally. We both know what they mean. I went through terrible depressions for the first six months I was out, getting up crying, not knowing what I was crying for. I'm not the type of person that gets depressed. Sometimes I'm sitting worrying, trying to make ends meet, and I think, 'Yeah, I can understand. I can understand them going back.' In a moment of weakness I can understand.

I've been out for fifteen months. I'm on licence and will be for the rest of my life. For the first six months I had to see a probation officer every week, then every two weeks, now it's every three. They send reports off to the Home Office. Soon it will be down to once a month. If you want to go abroad you have to ask the Home Office. And you have to ask if you want to remarry. I'd live in sin rather than do that – that's too much to ask. You've got to be careful. You can't afford to get angry, I couldn't have a heated argument in the street, say. The other person could get as angry as they liked, but I'd have to be careful. It has happened, people have been recalled.

Some people say I coped with my sentence well compared to others. I don't know. If I hadn't had children out there, it would have been so much easier. That was the hardest thing of all. They said, officers and suchlike, 'You've been so strong.' I could conceal it, but inside I was suffering. Some girls have gone through a life sentence and it seems it hasn't affected them at all because they've just gone along with it. I fought against it. It did make it harder, but it was the only way I could survive. I've got a really loving family – but all those years. . . .

I'm a different person. I've got to be different. You can't come out the same person you went in. Too much has happened, far too much heartache.

Conclusion

The women whose stories make up this book are not extreme, nor are they unusual. There are many thousands of women whose lives have followed a similar route. Some have dared to assume that they could have the same freedom as their brothers or male friends to roam the streets, sleep around and be 'stroppy'. Others have experienced disruptive, chaotic childhoods, foster homes, council care and approved schools. Any woman whose appearance or behaviour somehow infringes the predominant white male view of womanhood and who brushes with the law is likely to find herself heavily penalised by the courts. Black women, women who choose not to marry, those who have many lovers or have left their husbands, those with children in care, lesbian women, homeless women and women addicted to alcohol or drugs are more likely to find themselves in prison than their more conventional white married sisters.

In a materialistic society where money means power, status is measured in terms of expensive clothes and possessions. Many women are forced to live on meagre state benefits because of high unemployment levels and lack of childcare provision. Others receive only the low wages paid for 'women's work'. Surviving such poverty becomes an exhausting and unending battle, with no realistic prospect of access to money or status. In most family situations where there is money coming in, the responsibility or opportunity to earn money is more often the man's, whilst the responsibility for making ends meet (and for carrying the blame if they don't) is usually the woman's. The pressure in all cases to keep up appearances is great. It is hardly surprising that the majority of offences committed by women are petty crimes, fraud, prostitution and theft, and that some women are forced to resort to various forms of hustling in order to feed and clothe their families or to acquire for themselves the power and prestige that money can buy. As Martia said, 'When you've got good clothes and things you feel better. You have more power, you feel more confident, and people don't look down on you.' Or as another woman told us, 'I don't like being a thief, believe me. It's caused me a lot of heartache. But you can't let your kids starve.'

For some women crime can also mean a break from a boring and monotonous life. As one woman who spoke to us said, 'It gave me the chance to have things I otherwise couldn't afford, but it wasn't just that. It was the buzz I got out of it. Stealing was my life – I was hooked on it.'

But the costs in human terms are high. Once in prison, women are subjected to a petty and punitive regime. Totally separated from the outside world and powerless to resolve any difficulties they have left behind, not only their own lives, but the lives of children and other dependants are disrupted or torn apart. Relationships with all those left outside are usually damaged, if not destroyed. This process is compounded by the minimal and inhibited contact allowed through short, supervised visits and censored mail. Feelings of depression and despair are magnified by not being able to telephone to find out if a sick child is better, to ask a vital question, to put a crucial point to a solicitor, or to be able to write privately.

Women surrender control of their daily lives as they enter prison. Decisions are made for them; they are treated like children. Prison life involves a constant battle for survival, and maintaining a personal identity is all-important. The mind-numbing monotony, the unbelievable pettiness and lack of control create an atmosphere of tension and despair. Women react in different ways, but none leaves prison unchanged.

All too often, women in such an anonymous, comfortless environment respond by turning their anger and frustration upon themselves. Self-injury is appallingly common. Frequently it leads to punishment, a move to the prison psychiatric wing or even transfer to a psychiatric hospital or one of the dreaded Special Hospitals like Rampton, Broadmoor or Moss Side – the ultimate threat, the ultimate dead end. Some women deal with the system by withdrawing, going into themselves or 'sleeping their time away'. Those who resign themselves to the situation can easily become institutionalised and this makes readjustment to the outside world even more difficult. Yet other women survive life in prison by fighting every step of the way, challenging decisions and pushing the prison system as far as they can. As Sue said, 'Some girls have gone through a life sentence and it seems it hasn't affected them at all because they've just gone along with it. I fought against it. It did make it harder, but it was the only way I could survive.' The inevitable result is that some women spend weeks or even months being punished. They are denied privileges and kept in solitary confinement in cells stripped of furniture, but they feel they are maintaining an independence of spirit, an identity essential in the uniform, dehumanising prison world.

There is, too, constant denigration by some of the prison officers, whose unenviable job as little more than 'turn-keys' offers them little satisfaction and makes many bitter and resentful. It is hard to imagine any other situation in which one group of women has almost total control over another group, and in which both groups are viewed from the outside world with such dislike and hostility.

Racist attitudes by white prison officers and staff are common. Given the closed nature of the prison system, they have licence to act largely as they please. The combination of this licence and the comparative powerlessness of the women prisoners frequently leads to racist abuse. Judging from the experiences of the Black and ethnic minority women we interviewed, there is less racial tension among the women prisoners themselves than in the outside world. This is not to say that there is no racism: the African women, in particular, complain of racism from other prisoners. But there could be two reasons for the apparently low incidence of racism among the women themselves. First, they all have a common enemy in the system itself. Secondly, the economic and social conditions which give rise to racism in the outside world are largely removed in prison. Whilst competition for status remains, the economic reasons for institutional racism simply do not exist, and without that institutional underpinning racism amongst individuals is not so common.

Some of the women declare strongly that they will not return to prison again: 'I've learnt my lesson', 'I've learnt the hard way', 'I don't want to be a crook or a thief all my life.' But release from prison brings its own problems. For many, life outside does not offer the eagerly anticipated freedoms so long dreamed about. As Margy said, 'It's when you get out that the problems really start.' Difficulties faced before imprisonment have usually multiplied by the time of release, so that many women return to worse predicaments than those they left. Ex-prisoners, dominated and infantilised throughout their sentences, often lack the confidence necessary to regain control of their lives during the crucial first weeks of freedom. Those who have survived that difficult time have told us that the lack of self-confidence remains even when other problems have been resolved.

In practical terms, many women face homelessness, and most return to poverty. Damaged relationships have to be repaired, and some find their ability to make new friendships has been affected. As Sharon pointed out, 'You are very wary. I always think that if someone tries to get close to me they must want something from me. My immediate reaction, whether it be a man or a woman, is to think the worst of them. They might be the nicest person, but prison has made me that way.' Women recently released from prison often face hostility from neighbours and suspicion from prospective employers. The education and work available in prisons does virtually nothing to provide women with new skills which will help them survive without crime.

The determination of women who have been in prison to

regain control over their own lives is born of the anger, frustration and bitterness engendered by the pettiness and oppression of the prison regime rather than of any encouragement or practical assistance within or outside prison. Sharon illustrated this when she said, 'The attitude they [the prison staff] have towards you is terrible . . . But one thing prison's taught me is to be very strong, and that I *am* a worthwhile person. Nobody likes to have their freedom taken away from them, but all the abuse and everything they threw at me – it just made me stronger each time.' And as Ginger said, 'People say that you can't change the system. If that was true we'd still be in Newgate on straw. So it does change. But it's got to be changed by the people they accuse of kicking the system.'

We hope that the accounts in this book become part of that process.

Appendices

WOMEN'S PRISONS IN ENGLAND AND WALES

On 5 June 1987, the certified normal accommodation in women's prisons in England and Wales was 1,576. The population stood at 1,714.

Askham Grange, Yorkshire
Askham is an open prison, a few miles outside York. It holds up to 134 women. Askham has a mother and baby unit taking children up to 18 months.

Bullwood Hall, Rayleigh, Essex
Bullwood is a closed prison and youth custody centre, taking between 120 and 140 women and girls. The prison is divided into five houses with women and girls housed separately.

Cookham Wood, Rochester, Kent
Cookham Wood is a closed prison, originally built as a remand centre for boys. There are up to 120 women there, mostly from South East England, although a quarter (30+) of the women are due to be deported after serving their sentences. These are African, Latin American, Asian and European women.

Drake Hall, Eccleshall, Staffordshire
Drake Hall is an open prison and youth custody centre. It holds about 250 women – 75 per cent adult women (i.e. over

21); 25 per cent youth custody trainees. Many women are serving fairly short sentences.

Durham – Women's Wing, Old Elvet, Durham
Durham houses a maximum of 39 women in a wing of the men's prison. It is a top-security wing housing the few women Category A prisoners in the country. The majority of women at Durham are serving long or life sentences and most of them will be transferred to another prison before release.

East Sutton Park, Sutton Valance, Maidstone, Kent
East Sutton Park is the open women's prison and youth custody centre for the south of England, taking about 80 women and youth custody trainees. The prison is an old country house with its own farm, extensive gardens and greenhouses.

Holloway, London
Holloway is the main women's prison and remand centre for the south of England. It has a population of about 415 women. Holloway has a number of specialist units, including a unit for 'difficult and disturbed inmates', the C1 psychiatric unit, and a mother and baby unit which caters for babies up to nine months old.

Low Newton, Durham
A remand centre for on average 40 women and girls. A few convicted women also serve short sentences at Low Newton, but those serving longer sentences are allocated to other prisons.

New Hall, Flockton, Wakefield
A remand centre and closed prison for women serving short sentences, New Hall was converted from a boys' detention centre in August 1987. It is staffed by male and female officers.

Pucklechurch, Bristol
A remand centre serving a large area of the south-west, Pucklechurch takes about 80 women and girls, including a few women serving short sentences.

Risley, Cheshire
A remand centre housing 131 women and girls. Risley is also an allocation prison, which means many women are only there for a short time.

Styal, Wilmslow, Cheshire
Styal is a closed prison, which takes adult prisoners and youth custody trainees. There are about 270 women there, including over 50 youth custody trainees. Styal was originally a children's home and the prison is divided into 15 houses. Many of the women here are serving relatively long sentences. Styal has a mother and baby unit for babies up to nine months old.

SCOTLAND

Cornton Vale, Stirling
Cornton Vale is the only women's prison in Scotland, though several of the men's prisons have small units for women on remand (usually accommodating two or three women). Cornton Vale serves as a remand centre, youth custody centre and prison for adult women serving short and long sentences. It accommodates about 220 women and girls.

NORTHERN IRELAND

Maghaberry, County Down
A newly built top-security prison which accommodates women and men in different parts of the prison. Maghaberry is the only women's prison in Northern Ireland. It takes both remand and convicted prisoners and has places for 56 women and girls.

GLOSSARY OF PRISON TERMS

AG – Assistant Governor
Every prison has a Governor, some a Deputy Governor and all have Assistant Governors. Assistant Governors often carry responsibility for particular wings or houses. They are therefore the governor grades with most frequent day-to-day contact with prisoners. Like the main Governors, they deal with applications from prisoners and often preside at adjudications on prisoners alleged to have offended against prison discipline. Under the new working arrangements for prison staff introduced in 1987 the rank of AG has been replaced by Officer Grade 5.

Applications
Applications have to be made by prisoners wanting to see the doctor, probation officer or governor. Applications made to see the governor may be about a wide variety of matters – from asking for an extended visit to queries about difficulties with letters.

Association
Association is the time when prisoners are able to mix with one another. During association periods, women can watch TV, play games, talk amongst themselves, bath, wash and iron clothes. Prisoners are not, however, entitled to association. It is a privilege which can be withdrawn if a woman is being punished for breaking rules or if there are staff shortages.

Block
'The block' is the punishment block in any prison. It may be a few cells on the ground floor of a wing, or an entire building, as at Styal (where it is known as Bleak House). Whilst in the block, women often have their privileges (radio, books, tobacco) withdrawn and have no association. The cells are bare, and at some prisons mattresses are taken out of the cells during the day.

Canteen
The prison canteen is a shop which prisoners are allowed to visit once a week. Tobacco, extra stamps, toiletries, radio batteries

and sweets are on sale and women can spend their meagre prison earnings. They are also allowed to buy items other than tobacco and stamps from their 'private cash' (or private spends), which is money they may have had when they were sent to prison or which friends or relatives have sent in. Prices are the same as or slightly higher than those charged in outside shops, which means that women can afford to buy little. Black women have additional difficulties because even when toiletries suitable for their skin and hair are available they are usually extremely expensive.

Exercise
The right to exercise is one of the very few entitlements a prisoner has. It usually amounts to walking round and round a yard or garden; organised games are not usually allowed during exercise periods. Women are entitled to one hour's exercise per day, but this can be reduced to half an hour if they are also able to have association or are working or going to PE. Exercise is also available only if weather permits, so during the winter many days may pass when women are unable to go outside at all.

Grass
An informer. A grass may be someone who has informed on others when she was arrested or may be a prisoner who tells tales on other prisoners to the officers.

NACRO
The National Association for the Care and Resettlement of Offenders is a large national organisation. Among its functions is the befriending of women in prison and the offer of assistance with employment or accommodation after release.

Nonce
A nonce is a prisoner whose offence make them unpopular with other prisoners. In women's prisons those classed by other prisoners as 'nonces' tend to be women who have killed or injured children.

Parole

Parole is a scheme whereby some prisoners are released under the supervision of a probation officer before their normal release date. They become eligible after serving a third of their sentence, or six months, whichever is the longer. Prisoners have to apply for parole and their cases are considered by a local review committee including the prison governor, a probation officer and a lay representative. The cases of long-sentence prisoners are also considered by the national Parole Board which includes judges, psychiatrists, criminologists and probation officers. Reports are prepared on the prisoner both by those involved with her in the prison and her home probation officer, but she is not allowed to attend any hearings and has to make any representations in writing. Decisions are influenced by the gravity of the original offence, the prisoner's record and conduct in prison and whether she has anywhere to go on release. Reasons for decisions made are not communicated to the prisoner so that the system is widely held to be arbitrary and unjust.

'Privileges'

This is the name given to anything which prisoners are allowed but not actually entitled to, including association, education, extra letters and visits, radios, tobacco and the use of the prison library and canteen. Long-term prisoners are sometimes allowed more privileges than short-term prisoners and these may include a cassette or record player, potted plants and a teacup and teaspoon. Privileges are often stopped temporarily as a means of punishment.

Reception

Reception is the area through which prisoners are 'processed' when they enter a prison. During the reception process, prisoners' identities and sentences are checked, they are strip searched, have a bath and receive a cursory medical examination. They are then issued with bedding and other basic items such as a toothbrush and are allocated a cell. The procedure is often very slow and women frequently spend hours waiting in the reception area.

Remission

Remission amounts to one half of any sentence up to and including 12 months and one-third of any sentence over 12 months (other than a life sentence, which has no remission). Unless they are granted parole, prisoners are therefore usually released after half or two-thirds of their sentence (depending on sentence length) has been served. The remaining part is remission and may be forfeited for any breach of prison discipline. Trivial offences often result in seven or fourteen days loss of remission; that is, the release date is postponed by seven or fourteen days. Far longer periods may be forefeited for more serious offences against prison rules. If a woman has lost some remission she can apply to the Board of Visitors to get that **'time back'**, and, if she has not been in trouble within the prison during the last six months, she may have all or part of her lost remission restored.

Screw

The prisoners' term for a prison officer.

Slopping out

Slopping out is the daily routine of emptying chamber pots. Most women's prisons do not have toilets in the cells so that at night (often from 8 p.m.– 8 a.m.) the only course open to prisoners is to use the plastic potties provided. Women find this a particularly degrading and embarrassing procedure. Frequent digestive and urinary problems result from women avoiding the use of potties altogether.

Strips

This can mean either stripped cells or 'special' cells. Women are put in the 'strips' if they are regarded as being disruptive or in danger of injuring themselves or someone else. They can be a normal cell with all furniture removed, or a specially adapted cell with a small concrete pillar for a stool and a concrete platform for a bed, usually with a mattress on it, although this is often withdrawn during the day. There is no other furniture: the chamber pot is sometimes made of cardboard. Women in stripped cells usually have their clothing, including underwear, taken away and are made to wear a **'strip dress'** – a gown made of virtually untearable fabric.

FURTHER READING

Bardsley, Barney, *Flowers in Hell: An Investigation into Women and Crime*, London: Pandora Press, 1987.

Carlen, Pat, *Women's Imprisonment: A Study of Social Control*, London: Routledge & Kegan Paul, 1983.

Carlen, P., Hicks, J., O'Dwyer, J. and Tchaikovsky, C., *Criminal Women*, Oxford: Polity Press, 1984.

Carlen, P. and Worrall, A. (eds), *Gender, Crime and Justice*, Milton Keynes: Open University Press, 1987.

Dobash, R.E., Dobash, R.P. and Gutteridge, S., *The Imprisonment of Women*, Oxford: Basil Blackwell, 1986.

Edwards, S., *Women on Trial*, Manchester: Manchester University Press, 1984.

Heidensohn, Frances, *Women and Crime*, London: Macmillan, 1985.

Mama, A., Mars, M. and Stevenson, P., *Breaking the Silence*, London: London Strategic Policy Unit. (Available from Women in Prison, below.)

Nic Giolla Easpaig, A. and E., *Sisters in Cells: Two Republican Prisoners in England* Ireland: FNT [Foilseacháin Náisiúnta Teoranta], 1987.

Peckham, Audrey, *A Woman in Custody*, London: Fontana, 1985.

USEFUL ORGANISATIONS

Black Female Prisoners Scheme
Brixton Enterprise Centre
444 Brixton Road
London SW9
Tel: 01–733 5520

CAST (Creative and Supportive Trust)
34B Stratford Villas
London NW1
Tel: 01-485 0367

Prison Reform Trust
59 Caledonian Road
London N1 9BU
Tel: 01–278 9815

Women in Prison
Cabin T
25 Horsell Road
London N5 1XL
Tel: 01–609 7463/607 3353

Women Prisoners Resource Centre
1 Thorpe Close
Ladbroke Grove
London W10 5XL
Tel: 01–968 3121